Intonation Pra

Intonation Practice

Ian Thompson

Oxford University Press

Oxford University Press
Walton Street, Oxford OX2 6DP

London New York Toronto
Delhi Bombay Calcutta Madras Karachi
Kuala Lumpur Singapore Hong Kong Tokyo
Nairobi Dar es Salaam Cape Town
Melbourne Auckland

and associated companies in
Berlin Ibadan

ISBN 0 19 453090 6

First published 1981
Fourth impression 1990

The author would like to thank John Eckersley
of the Eckersley School of English, Oxford for his
support and encouragement during the development
of this book.

Set in Compugraphic Univers Light by
T. H. Brickell & Son Ltd., The Blackmore Press,
Shaftesbury.
Printed in Hong Kong.

Introduction

Speaking has much in common with singing. In both singing and speaking we not only arrange vowels and consonants in a way that makes sense, but we also control loudness, speed, voice quality and pitch. *Pitch* is a musical word; in physics the corresponding word is *frequency.* A large drum, a long organ pipe, the notes at the left hand end of a piano keyboard and a man's voice have a low pitch; a small drum, a short organ pipe, the notes at the right hand end of the piano keyboard and a child's voice have a high pitch.

When we sing, we have a good deal of freedom with loudness and voice quality; by controlling these two features sensitively we give pleasure to ourselves and others. In some kinds of music we have almost equal freedom with speed, though in other kinds the composer decides the speed fairly exactly. When it comes to pitch, however, we have hardly any freedom: if we sing to an instrument or an orchestra we must sing the exact notes the composer wrote, otherwise we shall be accused of singing out of tune or even of singing a different tune. If we sing without accompaniment we can move the *absolute* pitch of the song by starting on a higher or lower note, but we must not change the *relative* pitch: in other words the melody of the song (up here, down there, right up here, no change there, back to the first note here etc.) never changes, even though the position of the whole song in our voice does change.

When we speak, though, we have equal control of these four features: loudness, speed, voice quality and pitch. These features do different jobs in different languages, and in many languages, including English, they are interconnected. When we speak of "stress" and "rhythm" we mean combinations of these features; but the rise and fall of the voice — in other words the change of pitch — we call intonation.

Now some people have a naturally quiet voice, some speak extra fast and some have a rough voice quality. Physiology and personality are the basis of these differences, yet the quiet speakers vary their loudness, the fast speakers vary their speed and the rough-voiced speakers vary their voice quality within their own limits. In the same way a man has a naturally lower voice than a child, but both vary the pitch of their voice within their own limits.

Even more significant than the starting or finishing pitch of an intonation tune is its direction. Whether a falling tune falls from the top of our voice to the bottom or from just above midway to just below midway, it is still a fall, and the hearer hears it as such. Whether a fall-rise happens high in the voice or low, and whether it is wide or narrow, it is still a fall-rise. Pitch matters, but *change* of pitch matters more.

One great difference between singing and speaking is that the melody of a song has a musical meaning that is often independent of the meaning of the words, whereas the intonation of our speech depends entirely on the meaning of what we are saying. To put it more precisely, the intonation of a sentence depends on the situation—who we are talking to, what we are talking about, what has been happening—and our attitude to what we are saying—urgency, casualness, surprise and so on.

For an example of situational intonation, which is intimately linked to stress and the question of old and new information, write the words "I thought it was going to rain" on a piece of paper and ask a native English speaker to take it to the window and say it on a rainy day. Tape-record what he says, if possible. Then wait for a sunny day and repeat the process. Compare the recordings. The reason for the difference is that on a rainy day "rain" is old information, whereas on a sunny day it is new.

For an example of attitudinal intonation, listen to a native English speaker angrily telling a disobedient child "Don't sit on that chair!" and then using the same words as a friendly warning to someone who does not realise that the chair is about to collapse.

Of course, we cannot draw sharp lines between these categories: in the case of "I thought it was going to rain" the speaker's disappointment or pleasure with the weather will affect his intonation, and in the case of "Don't sit on that chair!" the question of whether you are talking to a naughty child or a friend is a situational one. Linguists are a long way from agreeing about what is the basis of intonation, but the practical teacher and the realistic learner need not worry themselves too much with theory. As long as we realise that intonation is only one of a group of features that all interact, we are on the road to success. The exercises in this course give practice in word-linking, vowels in unstressed syllables and sentence rhythm, as well as in intonation and sentence stress.

The coloured symbol (the intonation marks over the printed dialogues) respects the following conventions:

a A *thick* line marks the most important stress in a sentence. Other degrees of stress are marked with *thin* lines.

b In real speech there are endless steps between high and low pitch, but we have simplified them to three: high, mid and low. The symbols are intended as a guide so that the eye can help the memory and the ear, but the most important thing is the tape.

c Because of personal variations from speaker to speaker, we have used

the symbol ⌣⟋ (or in its extended form ⌣⎯⎯⟋

for the commonest type of yes/no question, even though on different occasions the speakers on the tape may

actually say ⎯⟋ , ⌣⟋ or ⌣ , with no difference in

meaning or attitude.

d For the fall-rise heard in Hopes and Wishes, Warnings and so on, we have used

the symbol ⌢⌣ (or in its extended form ⌢⎯⎯⟋

in all cases, even though the little rise before the fall may sometimes be quite strong, and sometimes absent altogether.

The point of all these simplifications is to make the symbols easier to read and the pattern easier to remember.

How to use this course.

To the student

The exercises ask you to do three things: to listen, to repeat
and to respond. In real life, of course, you will always be
responding, sometimes to a situation and sometimes to
another person's words: your response may be a question,
an answer, a piece of advice, a warning, a word of thanks,
and so on. Now, the stress and intonation of your response
will depend on two things:

a the situation you see or the words you hear;
b your own attitude to what you say in response.

Listening practice is vitally important: when you open your
mouth to speak your own language, you can hear with your
mind's ear exactly how your words will sound. You have in
your head a perfect sound-picture of your language, born of
years of listening. In order to get a good sound-picture of a
foreign language — especially if you are already an adult
when you are studying it — you need to listen more
intensively and more *consciously*. When you do each lesson
in this course for the first time — or even the first three
times — feel free to do it as listening only, without repeating
or responding. When you feel really ready to work actively,
do so, but don't hurry it.

Repetition practice concentrates not only on stress and
intonation but also on linking words together without a
break, so that your speech will flow smoothly forward. Much
of this practice consists of short pieces of sentences, which
have no meaning alone. This practice must be taken
seriously, for it is muscular exercise of the same kind as
karate or playing the violin. It is hard work and there is no
short cut.

Response practice is more fun, as you must create
sentences of your own. Most of the response drills have four
phases:

1 The cue, followed by a ● , which is the signal for you to
respond.
2 Time for you to respond.

3 The right response, followed by a ■ , which is the signal for you to repeat.

4 Time for you to repeat.

Of course there are often many responses that are all equally right, and in such cases we have chosen the one that will be most useful in real life.

A few response drills have no phases 3 and 4.

Remember the tape is your servant. If it gives you too little time, stop it. Rewind not only after the lesson to repeat the whole lesson, but also *during* the lesson if you wish, in order to repeat a section. When you come to a piece you know really well, run the tape forward. The tape doesn't know what you need most. You and your teacher do know.

To the teacher

As many languages have intonation patterns — even systems — widely different from that of English, the student here is not presented with numerous finely-differentiated variants. We have instead chosen what appear to be the most generally serviceable tunes, maintaining their distinctness as far as is natural. Within the English-speaking world, of course, there is great diversity between one dialect and another in the tunes used, but the underlying *system* — that is to say the number of basic tunes and the principles of stressing and destressing — remains much the same. So if there are patterns on the tape that you find unacceptably different from those in use in the variety of English the student wants to learn, you can always use the same material from the book but substitute your own vocal cues for repetition and response.

Equally some exercises will be less useful to students of certain nationalities than others. If your judgement tells you that a certain section can be missed out, no harm will be done, as the broad headings (Greetings, Asking WH-questions etc) are relatively independent. In the early stages of work, listening is all-important, and the student who simply listens his way through a section or more without actively responding will not be wasting his time. After one or two such listening sessions, however, the student must be encouraged to work really hard at pronunciation, aiming at overall shape and rhythm, with good rhythm, rather than worrying too much about individual tricky sounds.

Greetings

1   Listen to David and Harriet:

Harriet	Hello, David.
David	Hello, Harriet.
H and D	Hello, Jo.

In this course, when Harriet and David speak to you, they will call you 'Jo'. In English-speaking countries the name 'Jo' is used for men *and* women. For women it is written JO and for men JOE, but the pronunciation is the same. Now when the speakers on this tape call you 'Jo', they want you to answer them. Listen again.

Harriet	Hello, David.
David	Hello, Harriet.
Harriet	Hello, Jo.
David	Hello, Jo.

Now David and Harriet are going to speak much more slowly, so that you can easily hear how the voice goes up and down. We call this extra-slow speech 'slow motion'.

Harriet	H e l l o, D a v i d.
David	H e l l o, H a r r i e t.

Now do that again, at natural speed:

Harriet	Hello, David. ■
David	Hello, Harriet. ■

2   If you do not know a person very well, it is better to say *Good morning*, *Good afternoon*, or *Good evening*. Listen to this:

David	Good morning, Mrs Hopkinson.
Mrs H	Good morning, Mr Matthews.

Harriet   Good afternoon, Professor Bannister.
Prof B   Good afternoon, Miss Gulliver.

Now it is your turn. You know Mrs Hopkinson, but not very well. Answer her.

Mrs H   Good evening, Jø. ●

Here is Professor Bannister. Answer him.

Prof B   Good morning, Jø. ●

3   Now listen to two close friends when it is time to go:

David   Ah! Here's my bus. Cheerio, Harriet.
Harriet   Cheerio, David.

Here they are again, in slow motion: be ready to repeat:

David   C h e e r i o, H a r r i e t. ■
Harriet   C h e e r i o, D a v i d. ■

Now back to normal speed: be ready to answer:

David   Cheerio, Jø. ●
Harriet   Cheerio, Jø. ●

In the same way:

David   Bye-bye, Jø. ●
Harriet   Bye-bye, Jø. ●

And for people you do not know so well:

Harriet   Goodbye, Mrs Hopkinson. ■
David   Goodbye, Mr Matthews. ■

Mrs Hopkinson would like to say goodbye:

Mrs H   Well, it was nice to meet you, Jø. Goodbye. ●

And so would Mr Matthews:

Mr M   Well, I must be going. Goodbye, Jo. ●

If it is bedtime, of course, you say:

Harriet   Goodnight, David.
David   Goodnight, Harriet.

This is used for close friends *and* for people you do not know so well.

David   Goodness! It's eleven o'clock at night. I must go. Goodnight, Jo. ●
Harriet   Here comes your last bus home, Jo! Goodnight. ●

4   As you know, we can often say the same thing in two different ways. For example: *It's starting to rain* and *It's beginning to rain.* The words are different, but the meaning is the same. The same thing sometimes happens with intonation. Listen and see if you notice the different intonations:

Harriet   Good morning, David.
David   Good morning, Harriet.
Harriet   Good morning, David.
David   Good morning, Harriet.
Harriet   Good morning, David.
David   Good morning, Harriet.
Harriet   Good morning, David.
David   Good morning, Harriet.

We use all of these with the same meaning and in the same situations. It is the same for *Good morning*, *Good afternoon*, *Good evening*, *Hello*, but it is *not* the same for *Cheerio*, *Bye-bye*, *Goodbye*, *Goodnight*. These four, used when we leave someone, are almost always spoken like this:

David   Cheerio, Jo.

Harriet   Goodnight, Jo.

5   When you meet someone for the first time, you say *How d'you do.* The other person replies in exactly the same way: *How d'you do.* It's not really a question, and it shouldn't sound like a question. Harriet is going to introduce you to her friend Alan:

Harriet   Alan, I'd like you to meet Jo.
Alan   How d'you do, Jo.

Let's practise that once in slow motion:

Jo   H o w   d ' y o u   d o,   A l a n. ■

At normal speed:

Jo   How d'you do, Alan. ■

Some people do without the name, saying just *How d'you do.* David would like to introduce you to his friend Colonel Reeves:

David   Colonel Reeves, I'd like you to meet Jo.
Colonel R   How d'you do.●

6   Now listen to this telephone conversation:

Harriet   Hello. Lyford 4242.
David   Oh, hello. Could I speak to Harriet, please.
Harriet   It's Harriet speaking.
David   Hello, Harriet. It's David here.
Harriet   Hello, David. I didn't recognize your voice.
David   I didn't recognize yours, either. It's a bad line.

Listen to the beginning again and be ready to repeat:

Harriet   Hello. Lyford 4242. ■

A little later David says:

David   Hello, Harriet. It's David here.

Let's practise that:

David   Hello, Harriet. It's David here. ■

Now your number is Lyford 3131. Harriet's going to ring you; and as you're near the phone you answer it after two rings:

(*you answer the telephone*)

Harriet   Hello. It's Harriet here. ●
(*you reply*)

We hope the conversation went like this:

Jo   Hello. Lyford 3131.
Harriet   Hello. It's Harriet here.
Jo   Hello, Harriet. It's Jo here.

Do it once more, just to be sure.

7   Notice these useful expressions using *See you* . . . .
They are common between close friends. Here are some to practise:

Harriet   See you tomorrow. ■
David   See you next week. ■
Harriet   See you after half-term. ■
David   See you at Christmas. ■
Harriet   See you the year after next. ■

Now tell Harriet you'll see her on Saturday. ●

Jo   See you on Saturday, Harriet. ■

Tell David you'll see him at the meeting on Wednesday. ●

Jo   See you at the meeting on Wednesday, David. ■

Thanks and apologies

8   Listen to Mr Watkins and his secretary, Miss Roke:

Miss R   Here's the letter from Mr Harris, Mr Watkins.
Mr W   Thank you, Miss Roke.
Miss R   Would you like Mr McGill's letter, too?
Mr W   No, thank you.
Miss R   Oh . . . shall I bring you the last year's accounts?
Mr W   Yes, please.

Listen again, repeating Mr Watkins's part. Notice the intonation of *Thank you:*

Mr W   Thank you. ■
Thank you, Miss Roke. ■
Thank you, Professor Bannister. ■

Do that last one again, starting at the end:

Mr W   . . . Professor Bannister. ■
Thank you, Professor Bannister. ■

9   Now notice the intonation of *Yes, please* and *No, thank you:*

Harriet   Yes, please. ■
Yes, please, David. ■
Yes, please, Mrs Hopkinson. ■
David   No, thank you. ■
No, thank you, Mrs Hopkinson. ■

If we do not want to be too formal, we usually say *No, thanks:*

David   More tea, Harriet?
Harriet   No, thanks.

David   More tea, Jo?●
Harriet Have some more cake, then, Jo. ●

In the same way, *Thanks* is not so formal as *Thank you:*

Harriet Oh, I posted those letters for you, David.
David   Thanks.
Harriet And I got you your tomatoes, Jo. ●

Of course, you could say: *Thanks very much* or *Thanks
very much indeed.* Listen and repeat exactly what you
hear:

Harriet Thanks very much indeed. ■

10 Go back to part of the conversation at the beginning of
section 7:

Miss R   Here's the letter from Mr Harris, Mr Watkins.
Mr W   Thank you, Miss Roke.
Miss R   Would you like Mr McGill's letter, too?

Notice that when Mr Watkins says *Thank you, Miss Roke,*
Miss Roke does not reply to his thanks. She goes on to
the next idea. In a situation like this, it would be
strange to say *Not at all,* because it is Miss Roke's job
to do things for Mr Watkins, and he says *Thank you* auto-
matically. But when someone is really grateful and thanks
you from the heart, you generally answer *Not at all.*

David   That's very kind of you, Harriet. Thanks very much indeed.
Harriet Not at all.

Now repeat exactly what you hear:

David   Not at all. ■

Make it long at the end . . . tal| | |:

David   Not at all. ■

We often use this as an answer when someone says something like: *Sorry I'm late* or *Sorry to disturb you.*

David	Sorry to telephone you so late, Harriet.
Harriet	Not at all, David.

11 Here is a situation. It is your birthday and friends are arriving at your house with presents. You open the door to Alan:

Alan   Sorry I'm so late, Jo. ●
Oh . . . and I've brought you a little present. ●
Not at all. Sarah couldn't come. I'm afraid, but she left a note for me to give you; shall I read it you? ●
Dear Jo, sorry about tonight. Hope to see you at my birthday party next month. Love, Sarah. You've got her address, haven't you? I'll write it down for you if you like . . . ●

12 Now practise some useful apologies. First of all, listen and repeat:

Alan   Sorry. ■
Sorry, Jo. ■
Sorry I'm late. ■
Sorry I'm late, Bob. ■
Sorry I'm so late, Bob. ■

Or if you are telephoning David after ten at night:

Jo   Sorry to ring so late. ■
Sorry to ring so late, David. ■

Now it is half past ten, and you have got to ring Professor Bannister: do not say *Hello,* say *Good evening.*

Prof B   *(answers telephone)* Hello. Ashbury 292. Bannister here. ●

13 In these next few exercises we shall give you a situation, and give you time for your answer. Then we shall give the correct answer and finally you will have time to repeat it:
1. It is very early in the morning. You are ringing a friend. What do you say? ●

Jo   Sorry to ring so early. ■

2. A friend is studying. You disturb her. What do you say? ●

Jo   Sorry to disturb you. ■

3. A friend is helping you to do something, and you feel a bit uncomfortable because you are taking his time: ●

Jo   Sorry to take your time. ■

4. Two friends are talking, but you have got something important to tell them. You interrupt them: ●

Jo   Sorry to interrupt you. ■

14 Now listen to these three short dialogues. In each one, someone says *Sorry;* and in each one the answer is different.

Alan   Hello, Sarah. Sorry to keep you waiting.
Sarah   Not at all.

Harriet Hello, David. Sorry to keep you waiting.
David   That's all right.

David   Sorry to keep you waiting, Alan.
Alan   I should think so too.

Here is the first one again:

Alan   Hello, Sarah. Sorry to keep you waiting.
Sarah   Not at all.

Alan is probably not late at all, and even if he *is* a
bit late it does not matter, so Sarah says *Not at all.*
Here is the second one again:

Harriet   Hello, David. Sorry to keep you waiting.
David   That's all right.

Harriet *is* late, but David does not mind.
Here is the third one again:

David   Sorry to keep you waiting, Alan.
Alan   I should think so too.

As you can hear, Alan's angry because David is late.
Now listen and repeat:

Sarah   Not at all. ■
David   That's all right. ■
Alan   I should think so too. ■

So and *too* are long. Practise them again:

Alan   I should think so too. ■

Here are three situations. You take part. Remember your
name is Jo.
Last night there was a noisy party until three in the
morning. You could not sleep at all, and you are tired
and angry now:

Alan   Sorry about the noise last night, Jo. ●
Jo   I should think so too. ●

Harriet has broken your favourite cup, but it was an
accident:

Harriet   Sorry about your cup, Jo. ●
Jo   That's all right. ●

You are expecting a telephone call from David, and he
rings at nine-thirty in the evening:

| David | Hello, Jo. It's David here. Sorry to ring so late. ● |
| Jo | Not at all. ● |

15　There is another way of saying sorry, using *I'm afraid* . . . :

| David | D'you know Sarah's address, Harriet? |
| Harriet | I'm afraid I don't, David. |

Repeat Harriet's answer:

| Harriet | I'm afraid I don't, David. ■ |

Here is another example:

| Mr W | Can you speak Spanish, Miss Roke? |
| Miss R | I'm afraid I can't, Mr Watkins. |

Repeat Miss Roke's answer:

| Miss R | I'm afraid I can't, Mr Watkins. ■ |

Here are more examples:

Mr W	Can you speak Ugdi? ●
Miss R	I'm afraid I can't. ■
Mr W	And do you know the capital city of Ugdistan? ●
Miss R	I'm afraid I don't. ■
Mr W	So you haven't been to Ugdistan? ●
Miss R	I'm afraid I haven't. ■

Be careful to join the words together:

| Miss R | I'm afraid I haven't. ■ |

16　Now why do we sometimes say *I'm afraid* . . . and sometimes *I'm sorry* . . . ? Listen to this conversation in a shop:

| Customer | D'you sell garden tools, please? |

Shopkeeper	I'm afraid we can't help you, sir.
Customer	Any idea where I should try?
Shopkeeper	What about Cook's in the Market Place?
Customer	That's an idea. I'll go down there now. Many thanks.
Shopkeeper	Well, I'm sorry we can't help you.
Customer	That's quite all right. Cheerio.

Here is one more example:

David	Come in, Harriet. I'm afraid it's rather cold in here today.
Harriet	It is, isn't it? Are you having trouble with the heating?
David	Mmm. These things always happen in January, don't the
Harriet	Oh, well! That's life. I'll keep my coat on, I think.
David	Good idea. Sorry it's so cold. Anyway, they're coming to repair it tomorrow.

As you see, we use *I'm afraid* to introduce new information. In the shop dialogue, the shopkeeper answers th customer's question with *I'm afraid we can't help you, sir. We can't help you* is important new information. But at the end of the dialogue the shopkeeper repeats *we can't help you, I'm sorry we can't help you* which is now old information. It does not say anything new. The important thing now is that the shopkeeper is sorry. In the second dialogue David told Harriet before she came in that it was cold in the house. This was new information to Harriet, because David's house is usually warm in winter. But a little while later David repeats that the house is cold, although they both know it, because he wants to remind Harriet that he is sorry to invite her into a cold house. Listen again to both dialogues and be ready to repeat.

17 Remember that *Excuse me* is *not* the same as *Sorry*. Listen to this dialogue:

| Sarah | Where is the station? Can you find it on your map, Alan? |

Alan	No, I can't. Let's ask someone.
Sarah	What about that man across the road? He might know.
Alan	Good idea. Excuse me! Excuse me. Could you tell me the way to the station, please?
Man	I'm sorry! I'm a stranger here myself.
Alan	Oh. Thanks very much all the same.
Sarah	Hey! That girl running in front of us: she's just dropped something. Excuse me!!!
Alan	No. She didn't hear . . . Hey! It's a railway ticket. I'll put it in my pocket.
Sarah	Come on. We can catch her if we run . . . Hey!! Excuse me! You've dropped this!
Girl	What's that? Oh! Oh, my ticket! I'm most grateful!
Sarah	We called you just back there, but you didn't hear.
Girl	Well, I was hurrying to catch a train, but I think I've missed it anyway. I'll get the next one.
Alan	So you're going to the station? What luck!
Sarah	We're going there, too, but we couldn't find it.
Girl	Oh, it's not far from here. Well, I'm glad I can help you. You've certainly helped me!

18 As you heard, we use *Excuse me* to get someone's attention. We use it in restaurants when we want the waiter, for example. We never snap our fingers or clap our hands. Listen to David and Harriet in the White Horse Cafe:

David	Excuse me.
Waiter	Yes, sir?
David	We'd like two tomato soups, please . . .
Waiter	Two tomato soups . . .
Harriet	. . . and two mushroom omelettes, please.
Waiter	Certainly, madam.

Listen again, repeating David's part *and* Harriet's part.

Here is more practice, with names and without names.

David   Excuse me. ■
         Excuse me, Mr Watkins. ■
         Excuse me, Professor Bannister. ■
         Excuse me, please. ■

19   Notice that we use *Excuse me* only to get the other
         person's attention. Do not use it if the other person
         already knows that you want to speak. Between friends
         use *Hey!* Listen again:

Sarah   Hey! That girl running in front of us: she's just dropped
         something. Excuse me!!!

Alan   No. She didn't hear . . . Hey! It's a railway ticket. I'll
         put it in my pocket.

         Although Sarah is already listening, Alan uses *Hey!* to
         show his surprise. We sometimes use *Hey!* to people we
         do not know, if the matter is very urgent:

Sarah   Hey! S'euse me! You've dropped this!

         So what do you say to someone if you see his coat
         burning? Catch his attention and tell him his coat is
         burning: ●

Jo   Hey!! Your coat's burning! ■

         And if someone is going to cross the road without
         looking, tell him to wait for that car: ●

Jo   Hey!! Wait for that car! ■

         Lastly, someone gets off a train but he leaves his
         umbrella on the seat. Tell him he has forgotten his
         umbrella: ●

Jo   Hey!! You've forgotten your umbrella! ■

Congratulations, sympathy and surprise

20 Alan has just seen Sarah across the street. He wants to tell her something rather important:

Alan   Hey! Sarah!

Sarah   Hello, Alan. Nice to see you.

Alan   And you. The results are out! The exam results!

Sarah   Really? But they usually come out in September, or even October.

Alan   I know. Anyway, you've passed your music exam! Well done!

Sarah   Never! I was sure I was going to fail. Well, well! And what about your physics?

Alan   Oh, I failed it. Still . . .

Sarah   You failed it? I'm sorry to hear that, Alan. That is bad luck.

Alan   Oh, it was my fault entirely. I did no work at all!

Now listen to this part again; and repeat what Sarah says:

Alan   The results are out! The exam results!

Sarah   Really? ■

Alan   You've passed your music exam! Well done!

Sarah   Never! ■

The big surprise for Sarah is that she passed her exam, so she says *Never!* Listen and reply using *Never!*

Alan   Hey, Jo! Bus and train tickets are going to be cheaper next month! ●

Harriet Have you heard the news, Jo? All students of English can have a free holiday in the USA. ●

Be careful of the pronunciation: the first part of *Never!* is quite short, but the second part is longer. When it is not such a big surprise, it is enough to say

Really? Listen and reply using *Really?*

Sarah	I'm learning Arabic, Jo! ●
David	Hey! Jo! It's Harriet's birthday on Saturday! ●

Of course, you can also show surprise like this:

Miss R	The new copying machine's here, Mr Watkins.
Mr W	Is it?
Miss R	But we can't use it till Wednesday.
Mr W	Can't we?

But we shall practise that in a later chapter.

21 Now listen to Alan again:

Alan	You've passed your music exam! Well done!

Here are Harriet and her father. Repeat her father's pa■

Harriet	Dad! I've passed my music exam!
Father	Well Done! ■
Harriet	I got ninety-two per cent!
Father	Really? Well done! ■

Now you answer these:

Harriet	Jo! I've passed my driving test! ●
Jo	Really? Well done! ■
David	Have you heard about the football match? We won, Jo! ●
Jo	Really? Well done! ■

22 Another way of congratulating someone is like this:

Harriet	Hey, Alan! I've passed my driving test!
Alan	Good for you!

Repeat that once more:

Alan   Good for you! ■

What do you say if Alan says this:

Alan   Jo! Harriet's passed her driving test! ●
Jo   Good for her! ■

Here is another:

Harriet David's got a new job, Jo. It's much better than his last job! ●
Jo   Good for him! ■

And another:

David   Have you heard the football results? The Brazilians have won again! ●
Jo   Good for them! ■

But what do we say if the news is not so good? Listen to Sarah and Alan again:

Sarah   What about your physics?
Alan   Oh, I failed it.
Sarah   You failed it? I'm sorry to hear that, Alan. That is bad luck.

Practise that once more:

Sarah   I'm sorry to hear that, Alan. ■
Alan   I'm sorry to hear that, Professor Bannister. ■

Here are one or two for you:

David   Hello, Jo. I'm afraid I can't come this evening. My brother's had a motor bike accident. ●
Harriet I don't feel well, Jo. I think I'd better go home. ●

23   Very often we start our sympathetic answer with *Oh dear*

Alan   Oh, dear. I'm sorry to hear that. ■

Now you try:

Sarah   Jo! Someone's stolen my bicycle. ●
Alan   My father's business isn't going well, I'm afraid. ●

When it is not so serious we often say *That is bad luck.*

Harriet   How did the swimming go, David? I'm sorry I couldn't come and watch you.
David   Oh, I won the first race, but I lost the second and third.
Harriet   Oh, dear. That is bad luck.

Repeat Harriet's words:

Harriet   Oh, dear. That is bad luck. ■

Now practise these:

Sarah   I ran to the station, but I just missed the train. ●
Alan   I telephoned the theatre, but all the seats were sold, so I couldn't get any. ●

24   Revise what we have done. Do not forget to use *Really?* and *Never!* when necessary.

David   There's a new language school in Oxford, Jo! ●
Jo   Really? ■
David   But you won't believe the name: it's called The Hippopotamus School of English! ●
Jo   Never! ■
Harriet   I wanted a job there, but I didn't get it.
Oh, dear. That is bad luck. ■
Harriet   But my sister applied, and she got it! ●
Jo   Good for her! ■

Reassurances

25   Reassurances are all those words and expressions that make the other person more comfortable, less worried. Here are a few common ones for practice:

Alan   Don't worry. ■
Never mind. ■
There's no hurry. ■
Sarah   It's quite easy. ■
It only takes a minute. ■
That's enough. ■

Listen and repeat Sarah's part:

Alan   Sorry to keep you waiting, Sarah.
Sarah   That's all right. ■
Alan   I couldn't get any real orange juice — only synthetic stuff.
Sarah   Well, that's better than nothing. ■
Alan   The trouble is — the shops are shut tomorrow.
Sarah   Never mind. ■

What does the dentist say when you are afraid it might hurt? ●

David   It won't hurt. ■

Or if you are afraid it might take a long time? ●

David   It won't take long. ■

And what do you say if you are going out for a few minutes? Tell everyone you will not be long. ●

Jo   I won't be long. ■

How do you tell a friend there is nothing to worry about? ●

Jo   There's nothing to worry about. ■

Now Harriet wants to tell you a secret, but is anxious;
try to put her mind at rest:

Harriet   There's something I'd like to tell you, Jo, only I'm
          afraid someone's listening. ●

Jo   No-one's listening. ■

Harriet   Are you sure? The other thing is — I'm afraid you'll
          tell someone. ●

Jo   I won't tell anyone. ■

Harriet   Or you might laugh at me. ●

Jo   I won't laugh at you. ■

Harriet   Well, in that case I'll tell you. You see, the other day
          I was at a party . . .

26   Very often, reassurances use the word *only*. Listen and
          repeat Alan's part:

Sarah   Do hurry up, Alan. We'll be late.

Alan   Well, it's only six o'clock. ■

Sarah   That means we've got to be there in an hour!

Alan   Well, it's only a birthday party. ■

Sarah   Yes, Alan, but it's your cousin . . . I mean, it's bad to
          turn up late.

Alan   Yes, but he's only a distant cousin. ■

We can also extend the last one.

Alan   Yes, but he's only a distant cousin of mine. ■
          Yes, but he's only a distant cousin of mine, Sarah. ■

As you can hear, there is more than reassurance here;
there is a bit of impatience, too. You are with Mr
Watkins, who sees a child throwing stones at the blank
wall of an empty house. A blank wall is a wall without
any windows. But it is only a blank wall and only an

empty house. And anyway, he is only a child.

Mr W Just look at that horrible little boy, Jo. ●

Jo Yes, but he's only a child. ■

Mr W But he's throwing stones at a wall. It's downright dangerous! ●

Jo But it's only a blank wall. ■

Mr W That's all very well, but it's the wall of a house. ●

Jo Yes, but it's only an empty house. ■

Now here are Harriet and David, expecting some visitors David does not like. Repeat Harriet's part:

David Oh, Heavens! The Hodnipps are coming tonight!

Harriet They're not coming till eight o'clock. ■

David In other words I've got to sit here for two hours dreading the doorbell.

Harriet Well, they'll be gone by half past ten. ■

David I don't know how I shall stand it!

Harriet They're not that bad, David. ■

We suggest you do sections 1-26 again. You may feel that this is not necessary but it is important to be able to say everything quickly and easily. Remember, more practice means more progress!

Yes/No questions

27 David had to go to Newbury today. He gets back at nine o'clock in the evening. Harriet opens the door:

Harriet Hello, David. I'll take your coat.
David Thanks, Harriet. Whew!
Harriet Are you tired?
David Mmm . . . a bit. Ooh! That soup smells good!
Harriet Are you hungry?
David I'm absolutely starving.
Harriet Did everything go well?
David Pretty well. Coo! Baked potatoes! . . .

Here are Harriet's questions again. Be ready to repeat:

Harriet Are you tired? ■
Are you hungry? ■
Did everything go well? ■

Now we would like to ask some questions with *Are you . . .?* Repeat the right answer when you hear it, too.

Alan Where can I get some orange juice? ●
Jo Are you thirsty? ■
David That omelette looks good! ●
Jo Are you hungry? ■
Sarah *(yawns)* ●
Jo Are you tired? ■
Harriet *(groans)* Get the doctor, Jo. ●
Jo Are you ill? ■

And what do you say to someone standing at a bus stop?

Jo Are you waiting for the bus? ■

Now, you have just found David's pen on the floor. He comes in, looking worried. He has lost his pen, remember: ●

Jo Are you looking for your pen? ■

28 Now listen to Miss Roke:

Miss R Good morning, Mr Watkins. Did you enjoy your holiday?

Here she is again. Be ready to repeat:

Miss R Did you enjoy your holiday? ■

Now ask some questions like that. What do you say to someone just back from a football stadium? ●

Jo Did you enjoy the match? ■

. . . and to someone just back from the cinema? ●

Jo Did you enjoy the film? ■

. . . and to someone just back from the theatre? ●

Jo Did you enjoy the play? ■

Now listen and repeat as we gradually lengthen that last sentence:

Jo Did you enjoy the play? ■
Did you enjoy the play you went to see? ■
Did you enjoy the play you went to see on Monday night? ■
Did you enjoy the play you went to see on Monday night, Professor Bannister? ■

Notice how the rising intonation in these sentences is spread out over more and more syllables. The strongly stressed syllable is still *play* and the gradual rise begins at the end of that word; the very last syllable of all takes the sharpest rise.
Do that long question again, building it up from the end:

Jo   Did you enjoy the play you went to see on Monday night Professor Bannister? ▪

29   Of course, the main stress does not *have* to be on *play*. It can be anywhere, according to the meaning. Listen to this:

David   I went to a play last night.
Harriet Oh. Did you enjoy it?
David   I did. I saw some people I knew.
Harriet Did you speak to them?

After you have repeated Harriet's questions in the section there will be some questions for *you* to ask:

Harriet Did you enjoy it? ▪
         Did you speak to them? ▪

Be careful to pronounce *to them* properly?

Harriet Did you speak to them? ▪

Now do these:

David   I found a banana on the kitchen table last night, Jo. ●
Jo   Did you eat it? ▪
David   There was a marvellous accordion at the market this morning, Jo. Very cheap. ●
Jo   Did you buy it? ▪
David   At that meeting yesterday, you know, a lot of questions came into my mind. ●
Jo   Did you ask them? ▪
David   I found on the last day of my holiday in Spain I had a lot of coins in my purse that I couldn't change into sterling. ●
Jo   Did you spend them? ▪

30   Now listen to Sarah and Alan:

Sarah   You really ought to give up smoking, Alan. It isn't good
        for you.

Alan   I know it isn't; but what about sugar and salt and butter
        and strawberries and . . .

Sarah   Are strawberries bad for you?

Alan   Well, I read that they were, if you ate too many. It was
        in Health News. Do you read Health News?

Sarah   Only if I can't find anything better.

        Here is Sarah's question again:

Sarah   Are strawberries bad for you?

        The most strongly-stressed word here is *strawberries,*
        because we are already talking about other things that
        are bad for you. The new, important idea is *strawberries.*
        Listen and repeat:

Sarah   Are strawberries bad for you? ■

        Here are a few exercises:

Alan   Well, Jo, lots of things are bad for you: potatoes, . . .

Jo   Are potatoes bad for you? ■

Alan   Mind you . . . there are plenty of things that are good
        for you, too. Apples, fish, grass . . .

Jo   Is grass good for you? ■

Alan   Oh, yes . . . according to the food experts. George, for
        example . . .

Jo   Is George a food expert? ■

        Notice that in these examples the meaning would be the
        same even if we added the word *too.* Listen and repeat
        what Sarah says:

Alan   Well, Jo, lots of things are bad for you: potatoes, . . .

Jo   Are potatoes bad for you, too? ■

Alan   Oh, yes . . . according to the food experts. George, for example . . .

Jo   Is George a food expert, too? ■

She means, of course:

Jo   Oh, yes. I knew Professor Bannister was a food expert, but I didn't know George was.

Here is Alan's question from the dialogue again:

Alan   I read it in Health News. Do you read Health News?

Here again, the meaning is:

Alan   Do you read Health News, too?

But he does not need to say *too,* because the heavy stress on *you* makes the meaning clear. Listen and repeat, remembering that words like *you, he, them* in English are often without stress and very short, but that they are sometimes very long, carrying a very heavy stress:

Alan   Do you read Health News? ■

31   In these next few exercises, Sarah asks you a question. Reply with *Yes,* and then ask her the same question, as in this example:

Sarah D'you like autumn, Alan?

Alan   Yes. Do you like autumn?

The first exercise is the example:

Sarah D'you like autumn, Jo? ●

Jo   Yes. Do you like autumn? ■

Sarah Have you been to Egypt, Jo? ●

Jo   Yes. Have you been to Egypt? ■

Sarah	Are you taking your exam in June, Jo? ●
Jo	Yes. Are you taking your exam in June? ■
Sarah	Did you spend your summer holiday camping, Jo? ●
Jo	Yes. Did you spend your summer holiday camping? ■

Of course, your answer could be much shorter, like this:

Sarah	Did you spend your last summer holiday camping?
Jo	Yes. Did you?

Repeat that once more.

Jo	Yes. Did you? ■

Here are some examples for practice:

David	Have you taken your books back to the library, Jo? ●
Jo	Yes. Have you? ■
David	Are you spending Easter at home, Jo? ●
Jo	Yes. Are you? ■
David	Hey, Jo! Did you see last night's programme on world agriculture? ●
Jo	Yes. Did you? ■

Now a warning: do not confuse *did you? have you?* etc. with the Echo-Questions, which are written in the same way but sound quite different. If you would like to compare them, go on to page 86.

32 The next exercise is a little different from previous ones. Here you are a reporter interviewing Mr Kent on his hundredth birthday. Ask him questions, and we will whisper the idea to you like this:

Alan	Ask him whether he feels a hundred.
Jo	D'you feel a hundred, Mr Kent?
Mr Kent	No, I feel about seventy-two.
Alan	Ask him whether he can remember his childhood.

Jo   Can you remember your childhood?

Mr Kent   Oh yes, I can remember it better than last week.

One important point: listen carefully for the most strongly-stressed word in Alan's prompt:

Alan   Ask him whether he feels a hundred.

Notice the falling intonation on *feels*. This is because the most strongly stressed word in the question is *feels*. Now you ask the questions and remember to stress the most important word in the question.

Radio Voice   And now, our reporter Jo interviews Mr Charles Kent, who celebrates his hundredth birthday today.

Alan   Ask him whether he feels a hundred. ●

Jo   D'you feel a hundred, Mr Kent? ■

Mr Kent   No, I feel about seventy-two.

Alan   Ask him whether he can remember his childhood. ●

Jo   Can you remember your childhood? ■

Mr Kent   Oh yes, I can remember it better than last week.

Alan   Ask him whether he got many cards this morning. ●

Jo   Did you get many cards this morning? ■

Mr Kent   Oh, there were hundreds. I haven't counted them yet. If any of those kind people are listening, I'd like to say thank you very much.

Alan   Ask him whether there was one from the Queen. ●

Jo   Was there one from the Queen? ■

Mr Kent   Oh yes, there was. I'm very proud of it. Well, I must go to bed now. Thank you very much. Goodnight. ●

Jo   Thank you, Mr Kent. Goodnight. ■

33   To finish this chapter, here are some very short yes/no questions. Listen:

Mr W	What was Switzerland like, Miss Roke?
Miss R	Switzerland?
Mr W	Yes. You went skiing there, didn't you?
Miss R	Skiing?
Mr W	Yes. With your boy-friend.
Miss R	My boy-friend?
Mr W	Well, y-yes. I mean, didn't you, I mean . . .?
Miss R	I assure you, Mr Watkins, that I have never been to Switzerland, I cannot ski and I have no boy-friend. This morning's post is on your desk.

Now repeat what Miss Roke says:

Miss R	Switzerland? ■
	Skiing? ■
	My boy-friend? ■

Here are one or two for you:

David	Hello, Jo! How did you enjoy Albania? ●
Jo	Albania? ■
David	Yes. Did you enjoy your mountaineering? ●
Jo	Mountaineering? ■
David	Mmm. Did Elizabeth enjoy it, too? ●
Jo	Elizabeth? ■
David	Sorry . . . how stupid of me. I meant your grandfather. Did he enjoy it? ●
Jo	My grandfather? ■

34 All the questions so far have ended like this:

⌐ or ___ ⌐ or ___ ___ ___ ⌐

But not all yes/no questions end like that. Listen to this dialogue and repeat Alan's part:

Alan	Come in, Sarah. Would you like some coffee? ■

Sarah	No, thanks, Alan.
Alan	Would you like some tea? ■
Sarah	No. I'm OK, thanks.
Alan	Will you have some orange juice, then? ■
Sarah	P'raps I will, then. Thanks very much.

And here is a detective talking to a woman. Repeat the detective's part:

Detective	Did you see anything unusual? ■
Woman	Not as far as I can remember.
Detective	Did you hear anything unusual? ■
Woman	No, I don't think so.
Detective	Did you notice a large green van parked in the street? ■
Woman	I'm sorry, I didn't.

In those cases, as you see, there is a series of questions all of the same form. The first one rises and the others fall. But even in these cases the rising intonation is often used for every question. It does not really matter. Here is a rather different kind of question:

Harriet	Did you come by bike, David, or did you walk?
David	Oh, I walked. By the way, that's a nice carpet. Is it Turkish or Persian?

Harriet knows that David always comes either by bicycle or on foot. He never comes by bus or by car. So which is it: bicycle or foot? Repeat what Harriet says:

Harriet	Did you come by bike, David, or on foot? ■

And David is not an expert on carpets, but he knows that Harriet's carpet is Turkish or Persian. One or the other. Which? Repeat David's words:

David	That's a nice carpet. Is it Turkish or Persian? ■

Now do these; be ready to think quickly:

Harriet	Mary's had a baby! Isn't it wonderful? ●
Jo	A boy or a girl? ■
Harriet	A girl! She had it at the weekend! ●
Jo	Saturday or Sunday? ■
Harriet	Saturday! At nine o'clock! ●
Jo	Morning or evening? ■

Or you could say:

Jo	Did she have it in the morning or the evening? ■

If you find it a little difficult to pronounce questions
that fall at the end, try to forget the question-mark.
Think of the sentence with a full stop at the end.

Answering yes/no questions

35 Listen and repeat:

Harriet   No. ■
Sarah   No. ■
Alan   No. ■

Now practise the word *No.* Listen to Mr Watkins and Miss Roke, and repeat Miss Roke's part:

Mr W   Were there any letters this morning?
Miss R   No. ■
Mr W   That's odd . . . Oh, before I forget . . . have you heard the news?
Miss R   No? ■
Mr W   Miss Roberts is getting married. Are you thinking of getting married at all, Miss Roke?
Miss R   No!! ■

Now take those cases one by one.

Mr W   Were there any letters this morning?
Miss R   No. ■

She is not surprised or angry or worried. She simply answers the question. Here are some longer ways of replying.

Miss R   No, there weren't. ■
No, there weren't, Mr Watkins. ■
No, Mr Watkins, there weren't. ■

Be very careful to get a clear fall on *No,* especially when something else follows:

David   Is it snowing?
Harriet   No, it isn't. ■

David	Did it snow yesterday?
Harriet	Yes, it did. ■
David	Was there any snow last year?
Harriet	No, there wasn't. ■ *(quietly)* I think I'll go and work upstairs.
David	Why? Are you busy, Harriet?
Harriet	Yes, David, I am. ■

Now give true answers to the questions you hear. Do not worry about names, but give the longer answer, such as *Yes, I do* or *No, I don't; Yes, I am* or *No, I'm not; Yes, she has* etc.

Alan	Hello, Jo. Come in. Have you met my parents? ●
A's father	Are you English, Jo? ●
A's mother	Oh, we thought you weren't. Have you been in Britain long? ●
A's father	D'you find it cold in winter? ●
Alan	Oh, come on. Poor Jo's heard those questions a thousand times before. Oh . . . can you speak Japanese, Jo? ●
A's mother	Only there's a Japanese friend we'd like you to meet and his Engl . . .
A's father	Have your parents been to Britain, Jo? ●

36   Now listen and repeat Alan's part:

Sarah	Alan!
Alan	Yes? ■
Sarah	Have you heard of Kosmokrat?
Alan	No? ■
Sarah	Well, you know all those satellites?
Alan	Yes? ■
Sarah	Well, it's a new Soviet one. Did you hear about the latest American one last week?
Alan	No? ■

When Alan says *Yes?* or *No?* he really means *Go on! Tell me more!* Try one or two:

David   Jo! Are you there? ●
          Well, d'you know a girl called Fral Puxman? ●
          Don't you? Well, you know the Niagara Falls? ●
          And you remember the exact height of the Falls? ●

37   Listen to this and repeat Miss Roke's part:

Mr W   Are you thinking of getting married, Miss Roke?
Miss R   No, I'm not!!! ■
Mr W   Is that the truth, Miss Roke?
Miss R   Yes, it is!!! ■
Mr W   Do you ever open my private letters, Miss Roke?
Miss R   Your private letters, Mr Watkins? No, I don't!!! ■

Mr Watkins has no right to ask such rude questions. Now you will hear some equally rude questions. Be ready to answer:

David   Are you drunk, Jo? ●
Jo   No, I'm not!!! ■
Sarah   Did you wash your face this morning, Jo? ●
Jo   Yes, I did!!! ■
Mr W   Have you been reading my letters, Jo? ●
Jo   No, I haven't!!! ■

Or you might say:

Jo   No, Mr Watkins, I certainly haven't!!! ■

38   So far, all our answers have been a clear *Yes* or *No*, but often the situation is more difficult. Listen to David and Harriet:

David   You're good at languages, Harriet. Those people in front of us . . . are they speaking Swedish?

Harriet	I think so.
David	Not Norwegian?
Harriet	I don't think so.
David	So they must be Swedish tourists.
Harriet	Not necessarily.
David	What d'you mean? Surely if . . .
Harriet	Well, don't forget they speak Swedish in part of Finland, too
David	Oh, I didn't realize that. Do they speak with a different accent from standard Swedish?
Harriet	I suppose so. I'm not really sure . . .

Here are Harriet's answers again:

Harriet   I think so. ■
          I don't think so. ■
          Not necessarily. ■

Practise that once in slow motion:

Harriet   N o t   n e c e s s a r i l y . ■

At normal speed:

Harriet   Not necessarily. ■
          I suppose so. ■

39   One important thing: English-speaking people often say
I think so even when they are absolutely sure. Here,
Harriet may be sure about the language, or she may be a
little doubtful. Anyway, she has had enough time to
think about the matter, and, as David says, Harriet
knows something about languages.
Later, though, Harriet answers with *I suppose so,* which
means 'Don't ask me: I'm not an expert', or 'I haven't
really thought about the problem'. Listen again, and
repeat Harriet's answers:

David   You're good at languages, Harriet. Those people in front of us . . . are they speaking Swedish?

Harriet   I think so. ■

David   Not Norwegian?

Harriet   I don't think so. ■

David   So they must be Swedish tourists.

Harriet   Not necessarily. ■

David   What d'you mean? Surely if . . .

Harriet   Well, don't forget they speak Swedish in part of Finland, too.

David   Oh, I didn't realize that. Do they speak with a different accent from standard Swedish?

Harriet   I suppose so. ■

Here are some questions for you to answer. Remember, if you know something about the subject, use *I think so* or *I don't think so;* if you do not really know much about the subject, use *I suppose so* or *I don't suppose so.*

Alan   Jo, could I learn your language, d'you think? ●

Sarah   Would it take more than six months? ●

David   Mmm. Is your language more difficult than Welsh, for example? ●

Harriet   By the way, are there any Welsh speakers living in your country, Jo? ●

40   Here are some more answers ending with *so* for you to listen to and repeat:

Alan   Is it going to rain tomorrow, Sarah?

Sarah   I'm afraid so. ■

Alan   D'you think we'll have better weather for the weekend?

Sarah   I hope so. ■

Alan   D'you think they'll cancel the cricket if it rains on Sunday?

Sarah   I expect so. ■

Here is one that does not end with *so:*

Alan   If they do cancel Sunday's cricket, d'you think they'll have it on Monday?

Sarah   I doubt it. ■
I doubt it, Alan. ■
I very much doubt it, Alan. ■

And here is yet another odd one:

Mr W   We've heard nothing from Marshall's, Miss Roke, yet we wrote to them three weeks ago. D'you think they're on strike?

Miss R   I shouldn't be surprised. ■
I shouldn't be at all surprised. ■
I shouldn't be at all surprised, Mr Watkins. ■

41   Negative answers generally have the same intonation:

Alan   Is it going to rain tomorrow, Sarah?

Sarah   I hope not. ■

David   D'you think Jo will have any problems living in Britain, Harriet?

Harriet   I don't expect so, David. ■

But very often instead of I'm afraid not people say I'm afraid not.

us Driver   Just a moment, luv.

Sarah   What's wrong? Can't I take my bike on a bus?

us Driver   I'm afraid not. ■

42   You will remember that when David said:

David   So they must be Swedish tourists.

Harriet said:

Harriet   Not necessarily.

Repeat that in slow motion; as you did before:

Harriet   N o t   n e c e s s a r i l y. ■

And at natural speed:

Harriet   Not necessarily. ■
David   Jo, does everyone in your country want to learn English?

Here are some more answers beginning with *Not:*

Sarah   Do your parents go to Scotland every year, Alan?
Alan   Not every year. ■
Sarah   But when they do go to Scotland, they always stay in the
           same hotel, don't they?
Alan   Not always. ■

In the same way:

Mr W   Didn't I write to Marshall's?
Miss R   Not as far as I remember. ■
Mr W   But aren't they on our list?
Miss R   Not as far as I know. ■

Now Harriet and David.

Harriet   Lost his job, did you say? Poor old George! D'you think
           he'll find another job easily?
David   Not at his age. ■

Harriet	Poor old thing . . . Ooh, David. Are you using your pen?
David	Not at the moment. ■

Here are some more examples for you to do. Remember you can use *Not as far as I remember.*; *Not as far as I know.*; *Not at the moment.*; *Not always.*

Sarah	Have I ever given you my address, Jó? ●
Alan	Isn't there some special connection between your town and Oxford, Jó? ●
Harriet	Sorry to interrupt you, Jó, but are you using your umbrella at the moment? ●
David	I s'pose it's always nice weather in your part of the world, Jó, isn't it? ●

43 Many answers like *sometimes, generally,* take the same intonation:

Sarah	Do your parents stay in the North of Scotland?
Alan	Yes, generally. ■
Sarah	D'you ever go with them?
Alan	Yes, occasionally. ■
Sarah	So you usually go away on your own?
Alan	Yes, usually. ■
Sarah	D'you ever go abroad?
Alan	Yes, sometimes. ■

But more definite answers like *always, never,* must take a fall:

Miss R	Do we ever export goods to the Kingdom of Cosgrovia?
Mr W	No, never. ■
Miss R	What about Olnia?
Mr W	No, hardly ever. ■
Miss R	Is that because of problems with the Olnian Government?

Mr W   Yes, almost always. ■
Miss R   Do they impose a heavy import tax?
Mr W   Yes, always. ■

44   So if the answer shows 0 or 100 or something very near to 0 or 100 then the intonation falls. But if the answer is somewhere in the middle, we use the fall-rise. These next examples show the same principle:

Harriet   What was the house like, David? Was it nice?
David   Yes, it was marvellous. ■
Harriet   Was the garden OK?
David   Yes, it was reasonable. ■
Harriet   Were there any apple trees?
David   Yes, there were lots. ■
Harriet   Plum trees?
David   Yes, there were a few. ■
Harriet   Was there an electric socket in most of the rooms?
David   Yes, in every room. ■
Harriet   What about washbasins?
David   Yes, in some of the rooms. ■

Try some for yourself:

Alan   Have you got any British friends, Jo? ●
Sarah   D'you spend your weekends at home? ●
Alan   D'you ever go out on Wednesday evenings? ●
Sarah   Do any of your friends smoke, Jo? ●
Alan   Can you see any trees from your room? ●
Sarah   Are you ever tired after an English lesson? ●

Look at the next dialogue. Notice the intonation of the words like *probably* and *definitely* which are used in the same way as we have just practised. Repeat the doctor's part in this short consultation:

Harriet	D'you think my shoulder'll be better by Friday, Doctor?
Doctor	Possibly. ■
Harriet	So it'll take a few more days, you think?
Doctor	Probably. ■
Harriet	So I'll have to cancel tennis on Wednesday, of course?
Doctor	Definitely. ■
Harriet	Will it be painful tonight, d'you think?
Doctor	Yes, it may. ■
Harriet	I imagine it'll be pretty stiff tomorrow morning!
Doctor	Yes, it will. ■

Practise again, extending the last two:

Doctor	Yes, it may. ■
	Yes, it may be painful. ■
	Yes, it may be painful tonight, Harriet. ■
	Yes, it will. ■
	Yes, it will be stiff. ■
	Yes, it will be stiff tomorrow morning. ■
	Yes, it will be stiff tomorrow morning, Harriet. ■

45 We have one more kind of answer that takes the fall-rise. Listen to Alan and Sarah, and repeat Sarah's part:

Alan	Are you free on Saturday, Sarah?
Sarah	Well, I'm free on Sunday. ■
Alan	Good. Sunday's OK. D'you like lions?
Sarah	Well, I like tigers. ■
Alan	Well, you know Longleat . . . the famous park full of wild animals?
Sarah	Well, I've heard of it. ■
Alan	Good. Well, I'm taking you there on Sunday.

Notice that this kind of answer often begins with *Well* . . . Here are Sarah's answers again, for practice:

Sarah	Well, I'm free on Sunday. ■
	Well, I like tigers. ■
	Well, I've heard of it. ■

Now listen to these two examples, notice the intonation difference in the answers. Why are they different?

Mr W	Miss Boke, d'you speak Portuguese at all?
Miss R	Well, I speak a little Spanish.
Mr W	Did you study it at school?
Miss R	No, I picked it up in Spain.

Notice the fall-rise on *Spanish* but the fall on *Spain*. Listen to two more examples, and repeat Mr Watkins's part:

Miss R	Did you say you once lived in Florida, Mr Watkins?
Mr W	No, in California. ■
Miss R	In Los Angeles?
Mr W	Well, not far from Los Angeles. ■

46   Now, imagine that you are the owner of a fruit shop. The only vegetables in your shop are potatoes. You do not sell any other vegetables; only potatoes. Also, you do not accept foreign money, but you do accept cheques The third point is that you are open on Sunday morning, but not in the afternoon.

Customer	Hello, Jo. D'you sell vegetables, by any chance? ●
Jo	Well, I sell potatoes. ■
Customer	Good. Oh, by the way . . . do you accept German marks?
Jo	Well, I accept cheques. ■
Customer	Fine. Ah, before I forget . . . are you open all day Sunday? ●
Jo	Well, I'm open on Sunday morning. ■

Asking WH—questions

47 WH—questions start with any of the following words: *who, whose, what, which, when, where, why, how.* Questions such as *how long . . .?, how old . . .?* are also WH—questions. Listen to a television interviewer interviewing Gloriette Harrod, the film-star:

Interviewer	Miss Harrod, a question on everyone's lips, I'm sure . . . how many films have you appeared in?
G Harrod	Why does everyone always ask me that?
Interviewer	Well, I read somewhere it was about a hundred and twenty.
G Harrod	Where did you read that? Come on . . . let's look forwards instead of backwards.
Interviewer	O.K. What's the title of your next film?
G Harrod	Who's asking the questions?
Interviewer	Well, I thought I was, but it . . .
G Harrod	No . . . that is the title: 'Who's asking the Questions?'

Repeat just the questions, and notice that they all fall. The fall may be at the end, or earlier in the question, but wherever it is, the end is low.

Interviewer	How many films have you appeared in? ■
G Harrod	Why does everyone always ask me that? ■
Interviewer	What's the title of your next film? ■
G Harrod	Who's asking the questions? ■

48 Here are some for you. You are travelling with Harriet in the car:

Harriet	Hey, Jo! There's a hitchhiker. Let's pick him up. Ask him where he's going. ●
Jo	Where are you going? ■
Hitchhiker	Faringdon.
Harriet	Oh. I wonder how long he's been on the road, Jo. ●

Jo	How long have you been on the road? ■
Hitchhiker	Since early this morning.
Harriet	My watch has stopped, Jo. Could you ask him the time? ●
Jo	What's the time? ■
Hitchhiker	Quarter to five.

Now you find the word *sprag* in something you are reading. Ask what it means:

Jo	What does 'sprag' mean? ■

Now you are at a bus station. You want the Lambourn bus but there are several buses standing there. Start your question with *Which . . . ?* ●

Jo	Which is the Lambourn bus? ■

You want to know where you can leave your luggage. ●

Jo	Where can I leave my luggage? ■

You want to know how often the British have a General Election. Ask how often the British have a General Election: ●

Jo	How often do the British have a General Election? ■

49	Listen to David and Harriet, and repeat Harriet's part:

Harriet	Where on earth have you been, David? ■
David	Why? What . . . Goodness! It's midnight!
Harriet	Why on earth didn't you telephone me? ■
David	Well, I'd no idea it was so late. Hey — there goes the doorbell!
Harriet	Who on earth can it be? ■

As you see, we can show anger or surprise by putting *on earth* after the question word. Practise it:

Harriet   Where on earth have you been? ■
            Why on earth didn't you telephone me? ■
            Who on earth can it be? ■

            So what do you say to someone who shows you a ship in a
            bottle and says:
            I did that myself! ●

Jo   How on earth did you do that? ■

            If a friend is laughing and you want to know why: ●

Jo   Why on earth are you laughing? ■

            If you see a strange-looking person coming to the door
            of your house, and you want to know who it is: ●

Jo   Who on earth is it? ■

50   Listen to Harriet and David again, and repeat David's part:

Harriet   I'm not having a holiday this summer, David.
David   Why on earth not? ■
Harriet   Well, I've told my boss I'm working right through the
            summer.
David   What on earth for? ■

            David's first response was *Why on earth not?,* but the
            opposite of that is not *Why on earth?,* which is
            impossible, because a question cannot end with *on earth.*
            Therefore we say:

David   What on earth for?

            Here are two for you:

Harriet   I won't have any strawberries, thanks, Jo. ●
Jo   Why on earth not? ■

Harriet   Well, I'm giving up fruit for a month. ●
            What on earth for? ■

51   Now what happens if you ask someone a WH-question,
            and you either forget or do not understand the answer?
            Listen to Miss Roke and Mr Watkins; repeat Mr Watkins's
            part:

Mr W   What did Shanks say in his letter? ■
Miss R   Well, he said he'd like to meet you in Newcastle at half-
            past two on Friday the seventeenth of October. He's
            coming by train, so he suggested the Station Hotel.
Mr W   Where does he want to meet me? ■
Miss R   In Newcastle.
Mr W   Oh, yes. What time did he suggest? ■
Miss R   Two-thirty.
Mr W   Two-thirty . . . What day did he have in mind? ■
Miss R   He was talking of Friday the seventeenth.
Mr W   Ah, of course. What month was that? ■
Miss R   October, Mr Watkins.
Mr W   I see. And how's he travelling? ■
Miss R   By train. He's coming down from Aberdeen.
Mr W   And which hotel did he suggest? ■
Miss R   The Station Hotel. I think you should go home and rest,
            Mr Watkins. You're obviously overtired.

            Here are some for you. First listen to a news item, and
            we will prompt you to ask some questions on it:

Newsreader . . . and now for some sport. Tarog Haldimst, the
            champion swimmer from Ordunia, has won a prize of
            £479.67½p for his record-breaking swim across the
            Pnoragi River. He did it in just 14 minutes 36.893 secon

            You cannot remember the swimmer's name. Ask for it to
            be repeated: ●

Jo   What's the swimmer's name? ■

And you cannot remember where he comes from: ●

Jo   Where does he come from? ■

How much did he win? You have forgotten that, too: ●

Jo   How much did he win? ■

Which river did he swim? ●

Jo   Which river did he swim? ■

And finally: How long did it take him? ●

Jo   How long did it take him? ■

Giving information

52 Sometimes we give information in answer to a WH — question:

David   What's the time, Harriet?

Harriet   Nearly nine.

David   Goodness! I thought it was about half past seven. Where did I put my pen?

Harriet   It's in the right-hand inside pocket of the jacket you left in the garden last night.

Sometimes we make a remark either just for conversation or to say something important:

Alan   Looks as if it's going to rain!

Sarah   Hmmm . . . Hey! There's a mosquito on your arm, Alan!

In all cases the word that carried the most important idea has a strong fall. Listen and repeat:

Harriet   Nearly nine. ■

It's in the right-hand inside pocket of the jacket you left in the garden last night. ■

So where should David go to look for his pen? Into the garden. Now here is Alan again, just making conversation:

Alan   Looks as if it's going to rain! ■

And Sarah with more than just conversation:

Sarah   There's a mosquito on your arm, Alan! ■

Now listen to these four short sentences:

Mr W   My watch has stopped.

David   The train's coming.

Miss R   The sun's come out.

Harriet   The kettle's boiling.

Notice how the noun takes the stress, even though the verb is equally important. Really, of course, both the noun *and* the verb are new information, but the noun is stressed. Here they are again:

Mr W   My watch has stopped. ■
David   The train's coming. ■
Miss R   The sun's come out. ■
Harriet   The kettle's boiling. ■

And if you can smell burning toast? ●

Jo   The toast's burning! ■

And if you can hear: *(telephone rings):* ●

Jo   The telephone's ringing! ■

Of course, you can also say:

Jo   There's the telephone. ■

or:

Jo   Telephone! ■

53   Very often we give two pieces of information in the same sentence; for instance a place and a time. Listen and repeat David's answer:

Harriet   Has your brother got any plans for a holiday, David?
David   Yes, he's going to France in September. ■

As you can hear, the time and the place are equally important. The question was very general: . . . *any plans for a holiday?* . . . so in the answer we give equal stress to *France* and *September*. Here is a similar dialogue:

Alan   Any news this morning, Sarah?
Sarah   Yes, there's been a bank robbery in Sheffield. ■

Now your sister is studying Arabic at university. Answer Harriet.

Harriet   What's your sister doing at the moment, Jo? ●
Jo   She's studying Arabic at university. ■

And you have just bought a record for your mother. Dav sees you coming out of the music shop:

David   That looks interesting, Jo. ●
Jo   Yes, it's a record for my mother. ■

54   Very often, however, one piece of information is more important than the other. In many languages the less important information must go at the beginning of the sentence and the more important at the end. This sometimes happens in English, too:

Sarah   Yesterday afternoon we cycled to Yattendon. ■

The place is more important than the time here, so *Yattendon* gets the stress.

Sarah   Yesterday afternoon we cycled to Yattendon. ■

But we can also turn the sentence round and still keep exactly the same meaning and stress. Listen and repeat:

Sarah   We cycled to Yattendon yesterday afternoon. ■

The stress still falls on *Yattendon,* but notice the rise on *yesterday afternoon.* Here is Sarah again:

Sarah   We cycled to Yattendon yesterday afternoon. ■

Now here is Alan:

Alan   I'll telephone you when I get home.

Listen again and repeat:

Alan   I'll telephone you when I get home. ■

Notice that this sentence can also be turned around:

Alan   When I get home I'll telephone you. ■

55   Here are some reversible sentences for you to practise.
You will hear the sentence with not-so-important information at the beginning, like this:

Harriet   In the fridge there's a bottle of milk.

You turn them round like this:

Jo   There's a bottle of milk in the fridge.

Now do these:

Harriet   In the fridge there's a bottle of milk. ●
Jo   There's a bottle of milk in the fridge. ■
Miss R   This morning Mr Black telephoned. ●
Jo   Mr Black telephoned this morning. ■
Sarah   If you like, you can leave your bags here. ●
Jo   You can leave your bags here if you like. ■
Harriet   Actually I've forgotten his name. ●
Jo   I've forgotten his name, actually. ■

Notice that the comma between *name* and *actually* does
not change the intonation:

Jo   I've forgotten his name, actually. ■
Miss R   Usually I arrive at eight thirty. ●
Jo   I arrive at eight thirty usually. ■
Sarah   At first I didn't believe it. ●
Jo   I didn't believe it at first. ■

56   As you see, the not-so-important information is often
an adverbial showing where, when, how or how often

something happens. Often it is part of a condition . . . *if you like; . . . if you've got time;* and so on. But it can als be a noun. Listen and repeat Harriet's part:

David	Here's the milkman, Harriet.
Harriet	Good! We need some milk. ■
David	Shall I get some cream, too?
Harriet	No, we've got some cream. ■
David	Blow! I haven't got any money on me.
Harriet	Here's some money! ■

In these cases the secondary information is sometimes a word repeated from the sentence before:

David	Shall I get some cream, too?
Harriet	No, we've got some cream.

Sometimes the secondary information is an idea that was suggested before, even if no-one actually said the word. What does a milkman bring? Milk:

David	Here's the milkman, Harriet.
Harriet	Good! We need some milk.

Here are some for practice:

Alan	Here's the baker, Jo. ●
Jo	Good! We need some bread. ■
Harriet	I'm just going round to the fish shop, Jo. ●
Jo	Good! We need some fish. ■
Sarah	Here comes the potato man! ●
Jo	Good! We need some potatoes. ■
David	I'm just popping round to the egg-shop, Jo! ●
Jo	Good! We need some eggs. ■

57 Now listen to Miss Roke and Mr Watkins. Repeat Mr Watkins's part:

Miss R	Instant coffee today, Mr Watkins, I'm afraid.
Mr W	Oh dear! I can't stand instant coffee. ■
Miss R	And here are your chocolate biscuits . . .
Mr W	Good! I love chocolate biscuits. ■

Here are some more possibilities:

Mr W	Ugh! I hate milk in my tea! ■
Miss R	Oh dear! I'm not very keen on tomato soup. ■
Mr W	Oh! I enjoy reading. ■
Miss R	Good! I'm interested in mathematics. ■

Now you answer in the same way, using the word or expression that expresses your real feelings. Here is another example:

Sarah	What's on TV, Alan?
Alan	Football – on all channels.
Sarah	Oh dear! I'm fed up with football.

Now do these:

David	We're having soup tonight, Jo. ●
Harriet	There's jazz on the radio, Jo. ●
Alan	Coming to the meeting, Jo? It's all about politics. ●
Sarah	I don't like this room. Everything's green: Green walls, Green ceiling . . . ●
David	We're all going swimming this afternoon, Jo. ●
Harriet	There's an advertisement in the paper here – they're looking for a good cook. ●

58 Sometimes the new, important information is right at the beginning of the sentence. Listen and repeat Miss Roke's part:

Mr W	I've got a pain in my shoulder, Miss Roke. Who would you recommend?

54

Miss R	Dr Green's the man to see. ■
Mr W	Dr Green . . . Mmm . . . Oh dear! How d'you open this drawer?
Miss Roke	This is the way to do it. ■

Now Sarah wants to go out for the day. Suggest Cambridge. The place to go is Cambridge.

Sarah	I've got a free day tomorrow, Jo. I want to go somewher I've never been. ●
Jo	Cambridge is the place to go. ■

A friend of yours called Margaret knows all about Cambridge. The person to ask is Margaret.

Sarah	Who could tell me something about Cambridge before I
Jo	Margaret's the person to ask. ■

Finally, a question of transport: the cheapest way to go is the bus.

Sarah	What about the trains to Cambridge? ●
Jo	The bus is the cheapest way to go. ■

Now listen to Harriet and David, and repeat David's part:

Harriet	I'd love to go to Australia, David.
David	Oh, my sister lives in Australia. ■

Notice that if David says *there* in place of *Australia* the rising intonation at the end is not so common. Listen and repeat:

David	Oh, my sister lives there. ■

But repeating the words *in Australia* at the end of the sentence means: 'Come on — let's talk about it'. This way we can keep the subject open.

David	Oh, my sister lives in Australia. ■

Imagine your brother lives in Canada, Jo.

Harriet   We're thinking of going to Canada next year, Jo. ●
Jo   Oh, my brother lives in Canada. ■

Now imagine you neighbour is an engineer.

Harriet   I'd like to discuss this problem with an engineer, but I don't know one. ●
Jo   Oh, my neighbour's an engineer. ■

And your uncle knew Albert Einstein.

Harriet   I'm trying to read a book by Einstein — but it's difficult. ●
Jo   Oh! My uncle knew Einstein. ■

59   We use this intonation pattern in many sentences beginning with *I told you* . . . , *He said* . . . , *They promised* . . . , *I thought* . . . etc. In other words indirect speech sentences with the main verb in one of the past tenses. Here are two examples; repeat what Sarah says:

Alan   It's raining, Sarah.
Sarah   Mmm . . . They promised rain. ■
Alan   Well, they were right this time!
Sarah   I thought they would be. ■

And now repeat what Mr Watkins says:

Miss R   The new typist's just arrived, Mr Watkins. She's 5 minutes late.
Mr W   I thought she'd be late. ■

Listen for the /d/; it stands for *would*:
I thought she would be late.
I thought she'd be late.

Mr W   I thought she'd be late. ■

Now you were there, Jo, when they interviewed the new girl, and you thought she was not the right girl for the job. You thought she would be lazy, careless and rude.

Miss R   And she's so lazy, Jo. ●
Jo   I thought she'd be lazy. ■
Miss R   And you should see how careless her work is — thoroughly careless. ●
Jo   I thought she'd be careless. ■
Miss R   And the way she talks to visitors — she's so rude. ●
Jo   I thought she'd be rude. ■

We can also extend the last one.

Jo   I thought she'd be rude to visitors. ■

Now try some changes:

Jo   I knew she'd be careless. ■
I was afraid she'd be lazy. ■
I had an idea she'd be late. ■

One more situation: you are meeting a friend you have not seen for ten years. Will she recognize you? You hope so! So begin your answer with *I hoped . . .*

Harriet   Hello, Jo! You haven't changed at all! I recognized you immediately! ●
Jo   I hoped you'd recognize me! ■

But what would you say if she did not recognize you? Listen to Sarah meeting her cousin at the station:

Sarah   Hello, Jane! Nice to see you again after all these years!
Jane   I'm afraid I don't know you. I'm . . .
Sarah   It's Sarah! I hoped you'd recognize me!

Listen to that line again and repeat it:

Sarah   I hoped ~~you'd~~ recognize me! ■

As you see, the facts have changed, and so has the intonation. Listen to both cases again:

Harriet   Hello, Bill! You haven't ~~changed at all~~!

Bill   ~~I~~ hoped you'd recognize me!

Bill was right. She did. But now listen to this:

Jane   ~~I'm afraid I don't know you. I'm~~ . . .

Sarah   Hello, Jane! ~~It's~~ Sarah. I hoped ~~you'd~~ recognize me!

But Sarah was wrong. Jane did not recognize her.

60   Here are some more examples of what people say when they learn the truth about something, and that truth is different from what they had heard or thought before. In all cases the idea is 'I was wrong' or 'You were wrong'.

David   *(sound of brakes squealing)* God Almighty! . . . Oh, it's ~~OK~~: ~~nothing~~'s happened.

Harriet   Thank ~~God for that~~! ~~I was~~ afraid there was going to be a ~~terrible~~ accident!

Here is another:

~~ew~~sreader   ~~Good~~ morning. ~~This is Clifford~~ Fountain ~~with the News at~~ eight ~~o'clock on~~ Wednesday the ~~twenty-eighth of~~ May. ~~The Government are~~ . . .

Alan   Wednesday? ~~I thought it was~~ Tuesday!

And another:

Harriet   My brother's coming round today.

David   But ~~you~~ told me he was in Japan!

Here they are again:

David   God Almighty! . . . Oh, it's OK: nothing's happened.

Harriet   Thank God for that! ■ I was afraid there was going to be terrible accident! ■

Newsreader   It's Wednesday the twenty-eighth of May.

Alan   Wednesday? ■ I thought it was Tuesday! ■

Harriet   My brother's coming round today.

David   But you told me he was in Japan! ■

61   Now for a quick test to see how well you recognize the difference between the intonation pattern that means 'I was right' and the one that means 'I was wrong', but before you do it, we suggest you rewind and practise again. Here is the test. Listen to Mr Watkins and then answer the question:

Mr W   I thought it was going to rain.

Is it raining? ●   No.

Miss R   I was afraid today would be cold.

Is it cold? ●   Yes.

Mr W   I hoped the new calculator would arrive today.

Has it arrived? ●   Yes.

Miss R   They told me it was made in Holland.

Was it made in Holland? ●   No.

62   Now for some more contrasts between sentences that look the same when we write them, but sound different when we speak them because of the change in stress.
Imagine your favourite sport is badminton. You will hear a question, and you must answer with the words: *Badminton's my favourite sport.*

Alan   Jo, why d'you play badminton every evening? ●
Jo   Badminton's my favourite sport. ■

But what if someone asks you this question? Answer with
the same words!

Harriet   Which sport d'you enjoy most, Jo? ●
Jo   Badminton's my favourite sport. ■

Here is a very similar one: your favourite month is
September. So reply with the words: *September's my
favourite month.*

Alan   Why d'you always take your holiday in September, Jo? ●
Jo   September's my favourite month. ■

But if you hear this:

Harriet   Everyone's got a favourite month, Jo. Which is yours? ●
Jo   September's my favourite month. ■

And in the last one: *Cairo's the capital of Egypt.*

Alan   I've got a terrible memory — what's the capital of Egypt? ●
Jo   Cairo's the capital of Egypt. ■

But now for a different question:

Harriet   My geography's dreadful — where's Cairo? ●
Jo   Cairo's the capital of Egypt. ■

Now, if you had any difficulty with these, go back and
do sections 52-55 again. For speakers of many
languages, this is a very tricky part of learning English.
It needs time and practice.

63   Lastly something much easier: lists. Listen and repeat
Miss Roke's part:

Mr W   I've counted these three times, Miss Roke, and each time

I get a different result. Could you check them for me?

Miss R   Certainly. One, two, three, four, five, six, seven,
eight, nine, ten, eleven, twelve, thirteen, fourteen. ■

Mr W   Funny. There should only be twelve — one for each month
Anyway, would you put one in with each month's statistic

Miss R   By all means. January, February, March, April, May, June
July, August, September, October, November,
December. ■

You do the same with the days of the week. ●
And now the series beginning: First, second, third . . .
up to the tenth. ●
And the months of the year once more . . . ●

Invitations, warnings, orders and advice

64 An invitation can be in the form of a yes/no question. Listen to Sarah and Alan and repeat both parts:

Alan   Would you like to come to North Wales? ■
Sarah   I'd love to. ■
Alan   D'you fancy a bit of mountaineering? ■
Sarah   Yes, that'd be marvellous. ■

But invitations can also look like orders:

David   Hello, Mrs Povey. Come in.
Mrs P   Thank you, dear.
David   Take off your coat and sit down.
Mrs P   Well, I mustn't stop, dear. I shall get into trouble . . .
David   Well, ring and say you'll be late.
Mrs P   Well, as long as I'm no more than ten minutes.
David   Good. Have a cup of tea.

Notice that David does not say *Please come in*. For invitations between friends *Please* is not necessary; what *is* necessary is the proper intonation. Listen again and repeat David's part:

David   Hello, Mrs Povey. ■   Come in. ■
Mrs P   Thank you, dear.
David   Take off your coat and sit down. ■
Mrs P   Well, I mustn't stop, dear. I shall get into trouble . . .
David   Well, ring and say you'll be late. ■
Mrs P   Well, as long as I'm no more than ten minutes.
David   Good. Have a cup of tea. ■

How would you offer a cup of coffee? ●

Jo   Have a cup of coffee. ■

Or some more soup? ●

Jo Have some ~~more~~ soup. ■

65 You are giving a party at your house. Alan's voice will whisper the ideas to you. The doorbell rings.

Alan *(whisper)* It's Sarah, Jo. Let her in. ●

Sarah Hello, Jo.

Alan *(whisper)* I think she'd like to take her coat off. ●

Sarah Thanks.

Alan *(whisper)* You'd like her to come and meet everybody. ●

Sarah How ~~d'you do~~ . . . How ~~d'you do~~.

Alan *(whisper)* Offer her a drink. ●

Sarah I'd love one, Jo. ~~Many thanks~~. Ooh ~~— I must just go down to the phone box and make a quick~~ call. ~~I'll be back in~~ five ~~minutes~~.

Alan *(whisper)* Tell her to use your phone. ●

This is what we hope you said:

Jo Use my phone. ■

What do you say when someone says:

Sarah Bother! I've ~~lost my~~ pen. ●

Jo Use my pen. ■

Or:

Jo Use mine. ■

66 So far we have invited people to do this and that by ordering them to do something they enjoy. Sometimes orders are less enjoyable. Repeat the school-teacher's part in this scene:

Teacher *(amid hubbub)* Be quiet! ■ *(Hubbub continues)* Stop this noise at once! ■

Jinks   Please, Miss . . .

Teacher   Sit down, Jinks. ■   Open your books at page ninety-seven. ■

Jinks   Miss, I've left my book in the hall, Miss.

Teacher   Go and get it, then. ■

Do these, remembering that last one — *Go and get it, then.*

Jinks   Miss, the window's open, Miss. ●

Jo   Go and shut it, then. ■

Jinks   Miss, my shoes are dirty, Miss. ●

Jo   Go and clean them, then. ■

Jinks   Miss, I haven't done Exercise 3 yet. ●

Jo   Go and do it, then. ■

67   A rather differernt kind of order is used by the dentist. Repeat his part:

Dentist   Do come in, Harriet. ■

Harriet   Thank you.

Dentist   Sit down. ■

Harriet   Thanks. Shall I take my glasses off?

Dentist   No, leave them on. ■   Good. Now, open wide. ■

Harriet   Urglglub clugp glug.

Dentist   A bit wider. ■   OK. Have a rinse.

Harriet   Ah, that's better!

Dentist   There we are. Don't forget your coat! ■

Now you are the doctor. A man comes in who has hurt his elbow. Sarah will whisper some ideas when necessary, but first ask the patient in: ●

Patient   Morning, Doctor. I've hurt my elbow.

Sarah   *(whisper)* Perhaps he'd like to sit down. ●

Jo   . . .

Patient	Thanks.

Patient   Thanks.
Sarah   *(whisper)* He must roll up his sleeve. ●
Jo   . . .
Patient   I hope I haven't broken it!
Sarah   *(whisper)* Get him to bend his arm. ●
Jo   . . .
Patient   Ooh, that hurts.
Sarah   *(whisper)* Get him to straighten it again. ●
Jo   . . .
Patient   That hurts, too.
Sarah   *(whisper)* Ask him to raise it as high as he can. ●
Jo   . . .

Practice the pronunciation of that last one again:

Jo   Raise it as high as you can. ■

68   Parents and teachers talking to small children often use the same pattern. Imagine that Stephen is your little nephew. When he arrives at your house, tell him to wipe his shoes:

Stephen   Hello, Jo. ●
Jo   Hello, Stephen. Wipe your shoes. ■

He is spilling his orange juice. ●

Jo   Don't spill your orange juice. ■

And when he goes, he forgets his books. ●

Jo   Don't forget your books. ■

The intonation ⌐⁄ gives the listener confidence, But sometimes we need to point out danger, so we give a warning. Here are some warnings for you to repeat:

Harriet   Mind! ■

David   Careful! ■
Sarah   Look out! ■
Alan   Take care! ■
Miss R   Don't forget your gloves! ■
Mr W   Take a warm coat! ■

In every case the speaker is really saying 'If you don't, something will go wrong'. For example, *If you don't take a warm coat, you'll be cold.* Remember this connection between warnings and *if* sentences. Now you will remember that Alan invited Sarah to come mountaineering in North Wales. Listen and repeat Alan's part:

Sarah   I've never been to North Wales, Alan.
Alan   Well, bring a warm coat! ■
         Well, bring a warm coat with you! ■
         Well, bring a warm coat with you, Sarah! ■

Do that last one again, starting at the end:

Alan   Well bring a warm coat with you, Sarah! ■
         You know, Jo, Sarah doesn't always listen to my advice.
         I want her to bring some good strong shoes with her.
         Would you tell her, please? Remind her to bring some
         good strong shoes with her.●
Jo   Bring some good strong shoes with you, Sarah! ■
Alan   Thanks, Jo. The other thing is this: she'll need some
         good thick socks.●
Jo   You'll need some good thick socks, Sarah! ■
Alan   Just one more thing, Jo: could you remind her not to
         forget her gloves?●
Jo   Don't forget your gloves, Sarah! ■

69   Often it is hard to say what is a warning and what is a
         piece of advice. They can be difficult to distinguish.
         David has just decided he would like to learn an Eskimo

language. Tell him it is difficult: ●

Jo   It's difficult. ■
David Never mind, I'll get a job in Northern Canada.

Tell him jobs are not easy to find. ●

Jo   Jobs aren't easy to find. ■
David Well, I'll work as a forester.

Tell him foresters work extremely hard. ●

Jo   Foresters work extremely hard. ■
David Well, I could live with an Eskimo family on the ice.

Tell him he would find it jolly cold. ●

Jo   You'd find it jolly cold. ■

We can also extend the last one:

Jo   You'd find it jolly cold living on the ice. ■
      You'd find it jolly cold living on the ice, you know. ■
      You'd find it jolly cold living on the ice, you know, David. ■

Notice the long, slow rise after *cold:*

Jo   You'd find it jolly cold living on the ice, you know, David. ■

Many students find this a tricky pattern which needs a lot of practice. Your final piece of advice is:

Jo   I wouldn't go if I were you. ■

Sarah uses the same intonation when speaking to Alan, who is going to repair a faulty electrical switch, although he does not understand anything about electricity. The danger worries Sarah so she warns him not to touch it:

Sarah   I wouldn't touch it if I were you. ■

So what would you say to Sarah, who is just about to buy a very cheap camera? You know it will give her trouble: ●

Jo   I wouldn't buy it if I were you. ■

And how would you advise Harriet not to wear a pair of shoes that hurt her feet? ●

Jo   I wouldn't wear them if I were you. ■

And a positive one: David does not feel well. Advise him to go to bed. ●

Jo   I'd go to bed if I were you. ■

70   Suggestions in the form of questions take the same intonation as true questions. Listen and repeat Alan's part:

Sarah   Look at my hands, Alan. I got some paint on them yesterday and it won't come off.
Alan   What about using petrol? ■
Sarah   Yes, but how do I get the smell of petrol off?
Alan   Yes . . . Have you thought of paint remover? ■
Sarah   Paint remover, Alan? I'm talking about my hands, not the kitchen wall!

As you see, *What about using petrol?* starts high and falls, being a WH — question; whereas *Have you thought of paint remover?* has a sharp rise at the end, being a yes/no question. Suggestions beginning with *Let's* have the same intonation as Orders, and WH — questions. Listen and repeat:

Jane   Leave me alone! ■
Mr W   What's the matter with you? ■
Sarah   Come in and sit down! ■

Alan   Let's begin at page ninety-nine. ■

          Here are Harriet and David planning a trip to Scotland.
          Repeat Harriet's part:

David   When d'you think we ought to set off, Harriet?
Harriet   Let's leave on Friday afternoon. ■
David   Unless we left early on Saturday morning.
Harriet   Well, let's have a look at the timetable. ■

          Now you join in. Remember to use *Let's:*

David   Now you're the guest, Jø. Shall we go via Birmingham o
          via Peterborough? ●
Harriet   Shall we take sandwiches or buy a meal on the train? ●
David   And when we get to the Highlands — shall we hire bikes
          or shall we walk everywhere? ●
Harriet   Good idea. And uhh . . . Edinburgh. Shall we visit it on
          the way there or on the way back? ●

          Practise that last one again:

Harriet   Shall we visit it on the way there or on the way back? ■

          Now go back to the original conversation, and David's
          reply when Harriet said:

Harriet   Let's leave on Friday afternoon.
David   Unless we left early on Saturday morning.

          He is suggesting an alternative, another possibility.
          Listen again and repeat what David says:

Harriet   Let's leave on Friday afternoon.
David   Unless we left early on Saturday morning. ■

          Of course, this is a friendlier, softer suggestion than
          the following example, which is very direct and dominant
          and could cause a quarrel.

David   No, let's leave on ~~Saturday~~ morning.

Now, you are staying in a Bed and Breakfast with David and Harriet in Scotland when suddenly all the lights go out. It is only half past eight at night, but as it is September it is already dark. The others make various suggestions, but you have other ideas. Sarah will whisper your ideas:

Harriet   Goodness! It must be a power cut. Let's go and ~~ask for a candle~~.
Sarah   *(whisper)* Let's use Jo's torch.●
Jo   ~~Unless we used my torch.~~ ■
David   ~~I'd forgotten that.~~ Well, I s'pose the only thing now is to go to bed.
Sarah   *(whisper)* What about going down town?●
Jo   ~~Unless we went down town.~~ ■
Harriet   ~~It's a long way.~~ Are we walking?
Sarah   *(whisper)* Have you thought of going by bus?●
Jo   ~~Unless we went by bus.~~ ■

71   The same intonation pattern we have just practised is used by Miss Roke in the suggestions she makes to Mr Watkins. Repeat her part:

Mr W   How can we be sure these letters will arrive at Hobb's tomorrow?
Miss R   Well, I could always take them myself. ■
Mr W   Are you sure it's no trouble? Another problem: these daytime phone calls to Whiteshead in London are getting expensive.
Miss R   Well, you could always ring in the evening. ■

Notice that the highest point is on the *al* of *always*. Practise that once again:

Miss R   Well, you could always ring in the evening. ■

Now you and David are with Mr Watkins. He is telling you of a few of his worries, and he would value your advice. David just says what he thinks and you agree with him in general, but you do not want to be so direct. Here is an example with Harriet taking your part. Repeat what she says:

Mr W	You see, if Miss Roke leaves, what can I do for a new secretary?
David	Advertise!
Harriet	Yes, you could always advertise. ■

Now do these.

Mr W	But that takes so long. It's a problem of time.
David	Go to an agency. ●
Jo	Yes, you could always go to an agency. ■
Mr W	I s'pose I could. You see, the main problem is, I don't know whether she's thinking of leaving or not.
David	Ask her! ●
Jo	Yes, you could always ask her. ■
Mr W	Oh no, Miss Roke's very touchy — very sensitive.
David	Ask her indirectly. ●
Jo	Yes, you could always ask her indirectly. ■
Mr W	Well, if she says she is thinking of leaving, how can I persuade her to change her mind?
David	Offer her a rise! ●
Jo	Yes, you could always offer her a rise. ■
Mr W	But then everyone in the office'll want a rise!
David	Ask her not to tell anyone. ●
Jo	Yes, you could always ask her not to tell anyone. ■
Mr W	Well, I'm most grateful for your advice, but . . . I don't know . . .

Hopes and wishes

72 Listen to David and Sarah:

David   We're off to Portugal tomorrow.
Sarah   Well, I hope you get good weather.

Listen again and repeat Sarah's part:

David   We're off to Portugal tomorrow.
Sarah   Well, I hope you get good weather. ■

Here is David again, answer as Sarah did:

David   We're off to Portugal tomorrow, Jo. ●
Jo   Well, I hope you get good weather. ■

Now listen and repeat David's part:

Sarah   The only problem is Alan isn't feeling too well at the moment.
David   Well, I hope he feels better soon. ■

And now listen and repeat Miss Roke's part:

Mr W   My boy's going skiing with some school friends.
Miss R   Oh, I hope he enjoys it. ■

We can also extend the last one.

Miss R   Oh, I hope he enjoys his holiday. ■
Oh, I hope he enjoys his skiing holiday. ■

73 Here are a few for you. First, you are tired and you want to go to bed early. You hope no-one telephones you tonight. ●

Jo   I hope no-one telephones me tonight. ■

Next, you are working this evening and you do not want
to be disturbed: ●

Jo   I hope no-one disturbs me this evening. ■

Now, Sarah is taking her driving test tomorrow. You hope
she passes. ●

Jo   I hope she passes. ■

You are offering a guest some home-made ice-cream. You
hope it is not too sweet. ●

Jo   I hope it's not too sweet. ■

As you see, in this last example the fall-rise is all
on one short word: *sweet.* Try that one again.

Jo   I hope it's not too sweet. ■

Now offer your guest some coffee. You hope it is not
too hot. ●

Jo   I hope it's not too hot. ■

We can also extend the last one.

Jo   I hope it's not too hot while we're on holiday. ■
      I hope it's not too hot while we're on holiday in Portugal. ■

Do that one once more, building up from the end:

Jo   I hope it's not too hot while we're on holiday in Portugal. ■

74   Often we express hopes with *Let's hope* especially when
two people hope for the same thing. Alan is playing
football tomorrow and Sarah is hoping to beat her own
record in the long jump. It is dry today, but will it
rain tomorrow?

Alan   Let's hope it stays dry tomorrow. ■

Now you are on a train journey with a friend. You are
to change at Birmingham, where the train you are on now
arrives at nine o'clock. The train you want leaves at
four minutes past nine. You both hope you get your connection.●

Jo   Let's hope we get our connection. ■

And if you are walking in the hills with some friends,
but nobody has a map then you hope you do not lose the
way.●

Jo   Let's hope we don't lose the way. ■

75   Now listen and repeat Miss Roke's part:

Mr W   I seem to have lost my watch, Miss Roke.
Miss R   Well, +do hope you find it. ■

As you see, *I do hope* is stronger than *I hope* or *Let's
hope.* Notice the stress on *I do hope . . . — I do hope you
find it.* Here are Miss Roke and Mr Watkins again:

Miss R   My mother's not too well at the moment.
Mr W   Well, +do hope she's better soon. ■

You are in a fishing village, and the fishing boats have
gone out. A bit later a stong wind blows and the sea
gets rough. You hope the fishermen are OK.●

Jo   +do hope the fishermen are OK. ■

Now you are giving a present to a difficult aunt. Will
she like it? You hope so. ●

Jo   +do hope she likes it. ■

Lastly, you see a newspaper headline that says: DISASTER
HITS CAPITAL CITY. You hope it is nothing serious.●

Jo   +do hope it's nothing serious. ■

76   When you hope for something, it is usually possible, but how do you express a hope that you know will not come true? Really a dream more than a hope. Listen to Harriet:

Harriet   I wish I spoke Italian!

Does she speak Italian? ● No, speaking Italian is just a dream. Here she is again. This time repeat what she says:

Harriet   I wish I spoke Italian. ■

How here is Mr Watkins, worried about a business problem he does not know what to do.

Mr W   I wish I knew what to do. ■

We can also extend the last one:

Mr W   I wish I knew what to do about it. ■
         I wish I knew what to do about that letter. ■
         I wish I knew what to do about that letter from the tax inspector. ■

Now, Sarah and Alan have been staying at your house, and now it is time for them to leave. You wish they could stay longer. Tell them you wish they could stay longer.

Sarah   Well, Jo, we must be off now. ●
Jo   I wish you could stay longer. ■

And you wish they lived a bit nearer. Tell them you wish they lived a bit nearer.

Alan   Well, Jo it's a long way, so if we don't start now . . . ●
Jo   I wish you lived a bit nearer. ■

Unfortunately, you cannot stay with them next year. You wish you could.

Sarah   We've really enjoyed our stay, Jo. You must come and stay with us next year. ●

Jo   I wish I could. ■

77   Now something a little more difficult — moving the stress from one word to another. You see David repairing an electric clock. **He** knows how to repair electrical things, but what about you? That is a different story! You wish **you** knew how to repair electrical things.

David   There we are, Jo. Simple! ●

Jo   I wish I knew how to repair electrical things. ■

Did you get a good stress on *I*? Try it once more:

Jo   I wish I knew how to repair electrical things. ■

On another occasion you are talking about electrical things in general, and you agree that they are very convenient; the only problem is repair. You wish you knew how to **repair** electrical things.

David   Electricity makes life so much easier, and electrical goods really are relatively cheap to buy. ●

Jo   I wish I knew how to repair electrical things. ■

On yet another occasion you are successfully repairing a bicycle, because mechanical things are no problem to you, but **electrical** things are a very different matter.

David   You're making a marvellous job of that bike, Jo! ●

Jo   I wish I knew how to repair electrical things. ■

78   Sometimes we use *I wish* when we are a bit annoyed, like this:

Alan   Damn! I've just broken another glass!

Sarah   I wish you'd be more careful!

Notice that we use *would* here: *I wish you would . . .*

I wish you'd . . . I wish you'd be more careful. Here is Sarah again; this time repeat what she says:

Sarah   ┼wish you'd be more careful! ■

Now David and Harriet's next-door neighbour is singing and slamming doors at midnight.

David   ┼wish he'd make less noise! ■

So what would you say to yourself if you were trying to read and somebody nearby was whistling. Remember the word — to whistle. Stop whistling! ●

Jo   ┼wish he'd stop whistling! ■

Now you are waiting to hear a famous speaker, but the man introducing the speaker talks and talks. Stop talking! ●

Jo   ┼wish he'd stop talking! ■

Now you are on a camping holiday, sharing a tent with someone who snores. Stop snoring! ●

Jo   ┼wish you'd stop snoring! ■

And finally someone yawns! ●

Jo   ┼wish you'd stop yawning! ■

79   Another way of introducing a wish is *If only . . .* This expresses a very strong feeling, and notice that it is followed by a falling intonation. Miss Roke has just seen a wonderful secretarial job advertised in the paper. The only problem is — they are looking for a fluent Greek speaker. Repeat her part:

Miss R   ┼f only I spoke Greek! ■

And Mr Watkins badly needs a bigger office:

Mr W   ┼f only we had a bigger office! ■

If you are terribly busy, and want more time (but you know that is impossible) what do you say? ●

Jo   If only I had more time! ■

And if you like to live by the sea? ●

Jo   If only I lived by the sea! ■

And if you are desperately trying to get in touch with someone, but you do not know her address: ●

Jo   If only I knew her address! ■

You can use *If only . . .* in the same way as *I wish . . .* when someone is doing something annoying, and you want them to stop; do not forget to use *would.* So if a man near you is sniffing -- what do you say to yourself?

Jo   If only he'd stop sniffing. ■

80   Another case where we do not use the fall-rise intonation usual for hopes and wishes is when the sentence begins: *I hope to . . .* or *I wish to . . .* etc. Listen and repeat Mr Watkin's part:

Miss R   When d'you plan to be back from Bristol, Mr Watkins?
Mr W   Well, + hope to be back by Wednesday. ■

He could have said:

Mr W   Well, + plan to be back by Wednesday. ■

Or:

Mr W   Well, + expect to be back by Wednesday. ■

But, with no change in intonation, he says:

Mr W   Well, + hope to be back by Wednesday. ■

You are planning to spend a year working on a farm in

New Zealand. Begin your answers with *Well, I hope* . . .

Alan   Where are you going after you leave Britain, Jo?●
Jo   Well, I hope to go to New Zealand.■
Alan   How long d'you plan to stay?●
Jo   Well, I hope to stay for a year.■
Alan   A year? Hmmm. What are you going to do there?●
Jo   Well, I hope to work on a farm.■
Alan   That should be fun. Hard work, though.

81   Now listen and repeat the part of the angry customer in this restaurant scene:

Waiter   Yes, madam?
Customer   I wish to see the manager.■
Waiter   In what connection, madam?
Customer   I don't wish to discuss the matter. Kindly fetch the manager.■

This use of *I wish to* . . . is rather formal and official.
You go to the Rumanian Embassy to apply for a visa, and speak to a Rumanian Embassy Official:

Official   Good morning. Can I help you?
Jo   I wish to apply for a visa.■

Now there is someone at the door. He wants to see you, but you do not want to see him.

Harriet   *(whisper)* Nick's at the door, Jo.●
Jo   I don't wish to see him.■

More questions and answers

Question tags, short questions, echo-questions
and short answers.

82 To show you know what we mean by question tags, here
is an example:

Harriet It's the fifteenth today, isn't it?

And here is another:

David Terrible film, isn't it!

And another:

Harriet Don't forget, will you!

Isn't it?, isn't it! and will you!
These are all question tags. They always have a verb
like *be, have, must, can, do* — in other words the kind
of verb that can be the first word in a yes/no question.
Listen to David and Harriet, and repeat Harriet's part:

Harriet It's cold today, isn't it? ■
David Well, remember it's November.
Harriet Yes, but last November wasn't cold, was it? ■

Here Harriet is abolutely sure of herself, and she
knows that David will agree. Although these tags look
like little questions, they are not really. Harriet is
not asking David — she is reminding him. The conversation
continues:

David Well, last November was exceptionally warm, so they say.
Harriet We didn't wear overcoats, did we? ■
David Not in the first week, certainly.
Harriet Oh, yes, it got cooler later, didn't it? ■
David Quite a bit cooler — but not this cold.
Harriet There's been snow, hasn't there? ■

80   *More questions and answers*

83 As you know, the English love talking about the weather, so do some other nationalities, for that matter. Now you respond like Alan:

Stranger   Brrrrr.
Alan   ~~Yes, it is~~ rather cold, isn't it?

Repeat Alan's part again. Be careful! Do not make a break after *cold*. We see the comma, when it is written down but we do not hear it.

Alan   ~~It is~~ rather cold, isn't it? ■

• Now you do these:

Stranger   Brrrrr! ●
Jo   ~~It is~~ rather cold, isn't it? ■
Stranger   ~~And this~~ wind . . . ●
Jo   ~~It is~~ rather windy, isn't it? ■
Stranger   ~~And this~~ wet! Ugh! ●
Jo   ~~It is~~ rather wet, isn't it? ■
Stranger   ~~Yet you remember the~~ heat last summer? ●
Jo   ~~It was~~ rather hot, wasn't it? ■
Stranger   ~~But~~ d'you remember that ~~dreadful~~ fog ~~last December?~~ ●
Jo   ~~It was~~ rather foggy, wasn't it? ■

84 Now you are a doctor. Last month a patient came to you complaining of a cough, hiccups, tiredness and a very poor appetite, so you told him not to smoke, not to drink, not to overwork and not to eat sweets. Sarah will do the first one.

Patient   Morning, Doctor. *(coughs)* My cough's ~~no better.~~
Sarah   ~~You've been~~ smoking again, haven't you? ■

Now you do these:

Patient   Morning, Dr Jo. *(coughs)* ~~I've~~ still got this wretched cough. ●

Jo ~~You've been~~ smoking again, haven't you? ■
Patient *(hiccups)* ~~P'raps I have.~~ *hiccups)* ●
Jo ~~You've been~~ drinking again, haven't you? ■
Patient *(yawns)* A bit, Doctor. *(yawns)* ●
Jo ~~You've been~~ overworking again, haven't you? ■
Patient ~~I can't avoid it,~~ Dr Jo. ~~But my main~~ trouble is — ~~I've got no~~ appetite. ●
Jo ~~You've been eating~~ sweets again, haven't you? ■

85 The same falling intonation is used on *won't you* and *will you* after orders and warnings. Listen and repeat:

David Get here early tomorrow! ■
Get here early tomorrow, won't you! ■
Harriet Don't be late! ■
Don't be late, will you! ■
Mr W Try to be here at nine. ■
Try to be here at nine, won't you! ■

Now you tell young Stephen to wash his face. ●

Jo Wash ~~your~~ face, won't you! ■

And tell him not to forget his homework. ●

Jo Don't ~~forget your~~ homework, will you! ■

Now he is going out on his bike. Warn him to go carefully. ●

Jo Go ~~carefully,~~ won't you! ■

Warn him not to go too fast. ●

Jo Don't go ~~too fast,~~ will you! ■

Warn him to remember to look before crossing the road. ●

Jo Look ~~before crossing the~~ road, won't you! ■

And finally, three examples using that encouraging voice that doctors use — remember?

Doctor   Raise it as ~~high as you~~ can.

Now you are the doctor again, remind your patient to keep as warm as he can. ●

Jo   Keep as ~~warm as you~~ can, won't you! ■

And ask him to try to go to bed early. ●

Jo   Try to ~~go to~~ bed early, won't you! ■

And tell him not to forget his medicine. ●

Jo   Don't forget ~~your~~ medicine, will you! ■

86   Tags very often rise, too. Listen to Mr Watkins who is more than usually forgetful today, and repeat his part:

Mr W   ~~It's the 14th~~ today, isn't it? ■
Miss R   That's it.
Mr W   ~~I haven't~~ opened my letters yet, have I? ■
Miss R   Not yet, Mr Watkins, no.
Mr W   ~~You~~ said it was March, didn't you? ■
Miss R   No, Mr Watkins. ~~It's~~ February.

Now would you say Mr Watkins was sure or unsure? He was extremely unsure and so his tags went up:

Mr W   You said it was March, didn't you? ■

Now you will hear some questions about a man by the name of Reg: you think his other name is Hall, you think he lives in Winchester, you think he is a violin maker and you think he has got two sons who also make violins, but you are not quite sure.

David   This ~~chap Reg~~, Jo. Any ~~idea of his other~~ name? ●

Jo	It's Hall, isn't it? ■
David	Hall? Ah! Did someone tell me he lived in Hampshire? ●
Jo	He lives in Winchester, doesn't he? ■
David	And he's a craftsman, I'm told. D'you know what he makes? ●
Jo	He makes violins, doesn't he? ■
David	Is that it? Has he any sons and daughters? ●
Jo	He's got two sons, hasn't he? ■
David	Well you seem to know quite a bit about him. You don't happen to know what his sons do, by any chance? ●
Jo	They make violins too, don't they? ■

Of course, if you said the following, that was a good answer too:

Jo   They're violin makers too, aren't they? ■

87   All the tags so far have been negative-positive or positive-negative, for instance:

Miss R   You telephoned Australia, didn't you?
You didn't telephone Australia, did you?
Don't forget to ring Australia, will you?

But although negative-negative never occurs, we do find positive-positive tags:

Sarah	Guess who I had a letter from this morning!
Alan	Oh, so he's still writing to you, is he?
Sarah	Oh, it was nothing serious, Alan. Hey, when shall we go and see about our passports?
Alan	Let's go this afternoon, shall we?

Positive-positives always rise. Listen and repeat Alan's part:

Sarah   Guess who I had a letter from this morning!

Alan   Oh, so he's still writing to you, is he? ■
Sarah   Mmm. He wrote from Yugoslavia.
Alan   Oh, so he spends his holidays abroad, does he? ■
Sarah   Well, I think it's business, not pleasure.
Alan   Oh, so he's got a job over there, has he? ■

This kind of tag shows great interest and sometimes a little irony. Do these — and remember that the suggested answers that Sarah gives to Mrs Snobsley are not the only possibilities. Perhaps your answer was just as good.

Mrs S   . . . so one day, you see, I was talking to the Prime Minister, when suddenly . . . ●
Sarah   Oh, so you know the Prime Minister, do you? ■
Mrs S   Oh, yes, we're the greatest of friends. Anyway, someone told me my Rolls-Royce was parked in the wrong place, so . . . ●
Sarah   Oh, so you've got a Rolls-Royce, have you? ■
Mrs S   Oh, goodness yes. Always had one. I mean, every millionaire should run a Rolls! ●
Sarah   Oh, so you're a millionaire, are you? ■
Mrs S   I'm sorry! I really shouldn't talk about it. So anyway, I had a telephone call that evening at the Hilton, you see . . . ●
Sarah   Oh, so you stay at the Hilton, do you? ■

88   The other common type of rising tag is used as Alan used it a bit earlier.

Sarah   When shall we go and see about our passports?
Alan   Let's go this afternoon, shall we? ■

Now do these:

Harriet   Hey, Jo — shall we learn some Ordunian or shall we carry on with English? ●

Jo	Let's carry on with English, shall we? ■
Harriet	Shall we give up now, or shall we finish this lesson? ●
Jo	Let's finish this lesson, shall we? ■

Now here are some more where you can use your imagination more freely.

Harriet	*(pensive)* Jo! What shall we do if we fail our exam? ● How shall we go to Spain this summer? By air, by train or what? ● David and I are going, so are you, of course . . . Who else shall we invite? ●

Notice how we use *shall I?, shall we?* after *I'll* and *We'll:*

David	The Post Office shuts at five!
Harriet	We'll go straight away, shall we?
David	P'raps we'd better. Hey — is the back door open?
Harriet	I wonder . . . I'll go and check it, shall I?

So what would you say if someone said:

Grandpa	What a terrible noise, that music on the wireless! ●
Jo	I'll turn it off, shall I? ■

89 Now a word of warning: do not confuse question tags with true short questions which we looked at on page 27. Sarah and Alan are just coming out of a concert.

Sarah	I enjoyed that, Alan. Did you?
Alan	Yes, very much. But the fellow that wrote that second piece — I've never heard of him before. Have you?
Sarah	Well, I've heard of him, but that's all. I'm hungry. Are you?
Alan	Starving.

As you see, there is a change of subject: *I* and *you:*

Sarah   I'm hungry. Are you?

Repeat the following examples:

Sarah   I'm hungry. Are you? ■
         I've finished. Have you? ■

You meet Alan in the street and he says this:

Alan   Hello! You look tired.

You say:

Jo   Yes, I am. Are you? ■

Now do these:

Alan   Hello! Jo. You look tired! ●
Jo   Yes, I am. Are you? ■
Alan   A little. Have you been overworking? ●
Jo   Yes, I have. Have you? ■
Alan   A little! You'd like a holiday, I imagine. ●
Jo   Yes, I would. Would you? ■
Alan   Wouldn't mind one! Still, you get a Christmas holiday,
         I s'pose? ●
Jo   Yes, I do. Do you? ■
Alan   Well, a few days.

90   Next we will look at Echo Questions. Listen to Alan and
         Sarah again, talking about Sarah's tiredness, but in a
         rather different way:

Alan   Hello, Sarah! You look tired!
Sarah   Do I?
Alan   I think you've been overworking, you know.
Sarah   Have I?

If Sarah said *Really? Is that true? Oh?* the meaning
would be the same. Listen again and repeat Sarah's part:

Alan   Hello, Sarah! You look tired!
Sarah   Do I? ■
Alan   I think you've been overworking, you know.
Sarah   Have I? ■
Alan   If you asked your boss for a few days' rest, he'd say
        yes, I'm sure.
Sarah   Would he? ■
Alan   Of course he would. The office could manage without you
        for a day or two!
Sarah   Could it? ■

Here are some for you:

Harriet   You look well, Jo! ●
          Well, you looked a bit tired when I last saw you. ●
          I thought so, anyway. Oh, by the way, there's an exhibi-
          tion at the Town Hall. ●
          Mmm. A model engineering exhibition. There was one last
          year, actually. ●
          This is going to be the last one, apparently. ●
          So they say. They're not having one next year. ●
          Of course. I'm very sorry about it. ●

91   Sometimes we need to show more than just interest. A
         detective is interviewing Miss Roke about an office
         break-in:

Miss R   There's always a lot of money in the office safe, of
          course.
Detective Is there?
Miss Roke And we have quite a lot of visitors, as well . . .
Detective Do you?

88   *More questions and answers*

Miss R   Oh, yes, we do. And one of the typists has a boy-<u>friend</u>
          in a dynamite <u>factory</u>.
Detective Has <u>she</u>?

This intonation shows that Miss Roke is giving important new facts, of great interest to the detective. Listen
again and repeat the dectective's part:

Miss R   There's always a lot of money in the office safe, of
          course.
Detective Is <u>there</u>? ■
Miss R   And we have quite a lot of visitors, as well . . .
Detective Do <u>you</u>? ■
Miss R   Oh, yes, we do. And one of the typists has a boy-<u>friend</u>
          in a dynamite <u>factory</u>.
Detective Has <u>she</u>? ■

This is basically a falling pattern, but there is a
sharp rise before the fall. You will find that a rise-
fall like this always shows special interest, sometimes
with a bit of suspicion, irony or humour. If someone
reads you a rather ridiculous article from the newspaper,
how will you reply? Do the first one as Sarah does it:

Alan   Hey, Sarah! The King of Ordunia <u>wants</u> <u>to</u> in<u>vade</u> the Isle
          of Wight.
Sarah   Does <u>he</u>? ■

Now do these:

Alan   Hey, Jo! The King of Ordunia <u>wants</u> to in<u>vade</u> the Isle
          of Wight.●
Jo   Does <u>he</u>? ■
Alan   He's <u>sending</u> a hundred <u>soldiers</u>! ●
Jo   Is <u>he</u>? ■
Alan   They're <u>carrying</u> wooden <u>sticks</u> and <u>rifles</u>!●
Jo   Are <u>they</u>? ■

And sometimes this intonation shows that you are very impressed by someone:

Sarah   My younger brother's top of his class at school! ●
Jo   Is he? ■
Sarah   He always gets at least ninety per cent in exams! ●
Jo   Does he? ■
Sarah   He never forgets anything! ●
Jo   Doesn't he? ■
Sarah   He can speak very good French already! ●
Jo   Can he? ■

Or you could simply say:

Jo   Oh? ■

Or even:

Jo   Wonderful! ■
     Marvellous! ■
     Amazing! ■
     Fantastic! ■

92   As you see, these Echo-Questions look like questions, but really they are not. Now for something that does not even look like a question, and that is the Short Answer. Sometimes it answers a question, sometimes it agrees with a comment, and sometimes it disagrees with a comment. Listen and repeat Harriet's part:

David   We should come here more often. It's marvellous!
Harriet   We should. ■
David   Did we come up here last year at all?
Harriet   We didn't. ■
David   Haven't I told you the story of the old man that used to live in the woods up here?
Harriet   You haven't. ■

Practise those again one by one. Listen and repeat:

Harriet   We should. ■
           We didn't. ■
           +am. ■
           They can't. ■

Here are some for quick practice:

David   Cold, Jo, isn't it! ●
Jo   It is! ■
David   Still, it'll soon be spring! ●
Jo   It will. ■
David   We haven't had any really nice days this year yet
          though, have we? ●
Jo   We haven't. ■
David   Still, +s'pose we mustn't expect nice weather in March. ●
Jo   We mustn't. ■

93   We often add *Yes* or *No,* as we did on page 32, like this:

David   Yes, +can. ■
         No, they couldn't. ■

Be careful! There are two sharp falls here. Notice they are not:

Yes, +can or Yes, I can but

David   Yes, +can.

Now at natural speed. Make sure you join them together properly:

David   Yes, +can. ■
         No, +can't. ■

Here are some for you:

David You're studying English at the moment, Jo, aren't you?●
Jo Yes, I am. ■
David I imagine the intonation of your language isn't exactly the same as English intonation? ●
Jo No, it isn't. ■
David All languages are different in that way, I s'pose? ●
Jo Yes, they are. ■
David There aren't many Englishmen that speak your language really well, are there? ●
Jo No, there aren't. ■

94 Now listen to a rather different kind of short answer:

Teacher Now, who's been to France?
Stephen I have.
Teacher And did anyone go to Holland for the Flower Festival?
Linda Yes, I did.
Teacher And does anyone know how to count to ten in German?
S and L I do.

Here the important word is *I*. Repeat the short answers again:

Stephen I have. ■
Linda Yes, I did. ■
S and L I do. ■

If someone asked this question, what would you say? Who's Jo?

Jo I am. ■

And if your sister loves ice-cream, what do you say to this?

Harriet Does anyone here like ice-cream?●
Jo My sister does. ■

Here are one or two more:

Stephen Hey, I've been wondering about the sun and the moon.
Which one is nearer the earth?●
Jo The moon is.■
Stephen And which gives the earth its energy.●
Jo The sun does. ■
Stephen Oh. And who's older, Jo, you or me?●
Jo I am. ■
Stephen Who goes to bed earlier, Jo, you or me?●
Jo You do. ■

95 Now listen to Sarah and Alan:

Sarah Your parents both take sugar in their tea, don't they,
Alan?
Alan My mother doesn't.
Sarah Oh! I thought she did. And none of your family like
coffee, do they?
Alan I do.

Repeat Alan's part again:

Alan My mother doesn't. ■
I do. ■

Notice that the comment usually starts with *All* or
Everyone or *Everything* or *Both,* or else, *No* or *No-one*
or *Nothing* or *Neither.* The answer says 'Yes, you're
partly right, but you're partly wrong'. You have already
met this meaning for the fall-rise intonation on page 40.
Listen again and repeat Sarah's part:

Alan What about your parents, Sarah? Do they both smoke?

Sarah	My father does. ∎
Alan	Are all your family vegetarians?
Sarah	My brother isn't. ∎
Alan	And you say none of you has ever had stomach-ache?
Sarah	I have. ∎

Now imagine that you have been to Ordunia, you can speak the language and you know the Prime Minister of the country. But you cannot swim and you do not spend your summer holidays by the sea. A representative of the Ordunian Tourist Board is speaking to a group of potential customers at a reception.

Rep	Now, I don't s'pose anyone here's been to Ordunia, but it's a nice country. ●
Jo	I have. ∎
Rep	Really? I hope you enjoyed it. Nobody here can speak Ordunian, I imagine? ●
Jo	I can. ∎
Rep	Ah, well, that'll be very useful. Now, the Prime Minister, whom I'm sure you don't know, will be visiting . . . ●
Jo	I do. ∎
Rep	In that case we can probably offer you a very good job in our organization. By the way — everybody here can swim, I assume? ●
Jo	I can't. ∎
Rep	But still, I'm sure that you all spend your summer holidays by the sea, so you'll . . . ●
Jo	I don't. ∎

96 You will be relieved to know that there is only one more important kind of Short Answer, and that is the Contradiction. I say fizzy lemonade is good for you, and you say it is poison; in other words direct disagreement. Listen to Mr Watkins and Miss Roke, and repeat her part:

Mr W	Sorry to interrupt you again. They speak Spanish in Brazil, don't they?
Miss R	No, they don't. ■
Mr W	But you said the other day that all Latin America was Spanish-speaking.
Miss R	No, I didn't. ■
Mr W	Well, it doesn't matter anyway, because we never get any enquiries from Brazil.
Miss R	Yes, we do. ■
Mr W	Oh, dear! I seem to be getting it all wrong today!

Now you contradict your English teacher in the same way

Teacher	You're not taking your English very seriously, Jo. ●
Jo	Yes, I am. ■
Teacher	Well, I get the impression you don't practise outside the classroom. ●
Jo	Yes, I do. ■
Teacher	Well, if you ask me, you're wasting a lot of your time. ●
Jo	No, I'm not. ■
Teacher	After all, English is very important, I mean it's spoken in every country in the world, isn't it? ●
Jo	No, it isn't. ■
Teacher	Well, maybe not just yet, but national languages'll soon disappear, I mean, won't they, and then . . . ●
Jo	No, they won't. ■

Too, either, only, just and even

97   Listen to Alan and Sarah:

Alan   Does your uncle grow barley on his farm, Sarah?

Sarah   Yes. He grows red cabbage, too.

Now listen to David and Harriet:

David   Does your uncle grow white cabbage on his farm, Harriet?

Harriet   Yes. He grows red cabbage, too.

Did you notice the change of stress on *red cabbage?*
Listen again, and this time repeat Sarah and Harriet's
parts:

Alan   Does your uncle grow barley on his farm, Sarah?

Sarah   Yes. He grows red cabbage, too. ■

David   Does your uncle grow white cabbage on his farm, Harriet?

Harriet   Yes. He grows red cabbage, too. ■

Here is another; Mr Nichols, whose factory makes pickle,
is being interviewed;

terviewer   †understand you buy quite a lot of red cabbage,
Mr Nichols?

Mr Nichols   Yes. †grow red cabbage, too.

And another: this time the interviewer is questioning
Mr Nichol's cousin, Mr Wicks:

terviewer   Now your cousin grows quite a bit of red cabbage,
Mr Wicks.

Mr Wicks   Oh, I grow red cabbage, too.

The stress has moved again, twice. This time repeat Mr
Nichols and Mr Wick's parts:

Interviewer	I understand you buy quite a lot of red cabbage, Mr Nichols?
Mr Nichols	Yes. I grow red cabbage, too. ■
Interviewer	Now your cousin grows quite a bit of red cabbage, Mr Wi
Mr Wicks	Oh, I grow red cabbage, too. ■

Notice that in all these cases **too** stays in the same place. What moves is the stress: not only **bar**ley but red **cab**bage, too. Not only **white** cabbage, but **red** cabbage, **too**. Mr Nichols doesn't only **buy** it, he **grows** it, **too**. Not only Mr **Nich**ols, but his **cous**in, **too**.

Here are some for you to practise. The situation is this: you are interested in architecture — both traditional and modern — and you have been to both East and West Africa. You have not only travelled there — you have lived there, too. Here is Alan to ask you some questions:

Alan	So you've been to West Africa, Jo? (East) ●
Jo	Yes, I've been to East Africa, too. ■
Alan	Really? How marvellous — travelling in Africa! (Lived in Africa) ●
Jo	Oh, I've lived in Africa, too. ■
Alan	And you're interested in traditional architecture, I believe? (Modern . . .) ●
Jo	Yes, I'm interested in modern architecture, too. ■

98	If the idea is negative, *too* changes to *either*. Listen and repeat Mr Watkins's part:
Miss R	I'm wondering what's happened to our stock of postage stamps. We didn't send any first-class letters yesterday, did we?
Mr W	No, we didn't send any second-class letters, either. ■

Now do these:

Sarah	Jo — I know you don't like salt in your tea, but what about your coffee? ●
Jo	I don't like salt in my coffee, either. ■
Sarah	You don't like salt in your coffee? What about pepper? ●
Jo	I don't like pepper in my coffee, either. ■
Sarah	So you don't like pepper in your coffee? What about your brother? ●
Jo	He doesn't like pepper in his coffee, either. ■
Sarah	So what about his tea? ●
Jo	He doesn't like pepper in his tea, either. ■

99   Now listen to Harriet and David; repeat Harriet's part:

David	Is it true that Douglas makes gold watches?
Harriet	No, he only repairs gold watches. ■

Now listen to Sarah and Alan; repeat Alan's part:

Sarah	Is it true that Douglas repairs silver watches?
Alan	No, he repairs gold watches. ■

In the first case David was right about the gold watches,
but wrong about what Douglas did. *Make?* No: *repair!*
Listen to the first case again:

David	Is it true that Douglas makes gold watches?
Harriet	No, he only repairs gold watches. ■

But in the second case Sarah was right about repairing
watches, but wrong about the metal. *Silver?* No: *gold!*
Listen to the second case again:

Sarah	Is it true that Douglas repairs silver watches?
Alan	No, he only repairs gold watches. ■

Now do the next one:

David   Jo — does Douglas repair gold earrings? ●

Jo   No, he only repairs gold watches. ■

An acquaintance of yours called Alison is studying Economic Geography; nothing else. Not teaching — only studying. Practise the following:

Alan   So Alison's teaching Economic Geography too, is she? ●

Jo   No, she's only studying Economic Geography. ■

David   So she's studying Physical Geography, too, is she? ●

Jo   No, she's only studying Economic Geography. ■

Alan   What about Economic History? I imagine that comes into it, too. ●

Jo   No, she's only studying Economic Geography. ■

100   As you know, we often use *just* in the same sense as *only*. Listen and repeat Mr Watkins's part:

Inquirer   Are you pushing English cherries in your advertising campaign?

Mr W   No, we're just encouraging people to eat English apples. ■

Now you do these:

David   Hey, Jo! Is he encouraging people to eat Irish apples, too? ●

Jo   No, he's just encouraging people to eat English apples. ■

Sarah   D'you mean he's forcing people to eat English apples? ●

Jo   No, he's just encouraging people to eat English apples. ■

Practise that last once again because of the long tail of unstressed words; be sure to join the words properly too:

Jo   No, he's just encouraging people to eat English apples. ■

101   Here are David and Harriet again; repeat David's part:

Harriet   I've heard that Willie Grant wrote books on all subjects.
David   Oh, yes, he even wrote a book on Scottish trains. ■

And now Alan and Sarah; repeat Sarah's part:

Alan   I've heard that Willie Grant wrote books on trains all
          over the world.
Sarah   Oh, yes, he even wrote a book on Scottish trains. ■

And now Miss Roke and Mr Watkins; repeat Mr Watkins's
part:

Miss R   I've heard that Willie Grant was a great expert on
          Scottish trains.
Mr W   Oh, yes, he even wrote a book on Scottish trains. ■

Now you know an odd character who wears his overcoat
in the house. You will hear two questions, and your
answer will surprise the questioner:

David   Is it true that old Fred wears his overcoat wherever he
          goes? ●
Jo   Oh, yes, he even wears his overcoat in the house. ■
Sarah   I've been told that old Fred's house is freezing cold. ●
Jo   Oh, yes, he even wears his overcoat in the house. ■

Another acquaintance of yours speaks Chinese:

Harriet   Someone told me Rosemary speaks several languages. ●
Jo   Oh, yes, she even speaks Chinese. ■
Alan   You know Rosemary, Jo — is it true she can read Chinese? ●
Jo   Oh, yes, she even speaks Chinese. ■

And a very rich friend has bought a castle:

David   This fellow Stanley — he loves castles, so I hear. ●

Jo   Oh, yes, he's even bought a castle. ■
Sarah   What's all this about a chap called Stanley who goes
        round buying things? ●
Jo   Oh, yes, he's even bought a castle. ■

102   Sometimes *even* stands at the beginning of the sentence:

Miss R   This new typewriter — is it light in weight?
Salesman   Oh, yes, even a child can carry it.
Miss R   What about maintenance? Is it easy to repair?
Salesman   Oh, yes, even I can repair it.

           Practise those two once again:

Salesman   Even a child can carry it. ■
           Even I can repair it. ■

           Now you are the salesman:

Miss R   What about the price? No doubt a large office could
           afford one . . . ●
Jo   Oh, yes, even a small office could afford one. ■
Miss R   Good. Now I see that all your new typewriters have a
           guarantee, but what about your second-hand ones? ●
Jo   Oh, yes, even our second-hand ones have a guarantee. ■
Miss R   I'm glad to hear that. Now you say that your de-luxe
           model is extremely popular, but what about your standard
           model? ●
Jo   Oh, yes, even our standard model's extremely popular. ■

Index

The numbers refer to the sections in which the items listed below are practised.